P9-EMO-678

Los Braceros

Los Braceros

MEMORIES OF BRACERO WORKERS
1942-1964

compiled, annotated, and translated by

José Rodolfo Jacobo

foreword by
César A. González-T.

Southern Border Press

CREDITS

Creative Director: *Maria Ortega, José-Rodolfo Jacobo*
Designer: *María Ortega*
Production: *María Ortega*
Photo Research: *José-Rodolfo Jacobo & Rodolfo Arias*

ISBN 0-9749805-0-1 (pbk)

Dedication

Para mamá y papá

૨

Who like so many others left their homes and family
behind in search of a better life for their children.

Acknowledgements

This work is part of an endeavor to create an archive of *bracero* memories so that tomorrow the stories of our fathers and *abuelos* can be read by our children. The work is only the beginning of the larger more comprehensive archive we one day hope to achieve. This Bracero Oral History Project is very much a work in progress, and it would not be possible without the support and inspiration of so many individuals.

I would first like to acknowledge my mother and father who endured poverty and discrimination so that my brothers and I would have food on our table. ***Gracias mamá y papá por todo lo que nos han dado.*** I would like to thank Melanie for her support in all my projects and Isabella Itchel for being the light of my life. You Isabella, are my *Verbum Unicum*.

Thomas Davies, Richard Griswold del Castillo, Mike Ornelas, and César A. González-T.—you are my foundation as a scholar. Rodolfo Arias, Manlio Correa, David Vega, and Mario Martín— your friendship is invaluable. María Ortega thank you for all your hard work and dedication.

I also would like to express my gratitude to those who in one way or another helped this project move along— Karina Ruelas Miramontes, Frank Snook, Jim Tompkins-MacLaine, Vanessa Holanda, Cristina Rodríguez, and Stephanie Farrar. I would like to thank the Chicano Studies department and the Center for Latin American Studies for their support. Finally, I offer this work to all the women and men who plant and harvest our food.

José Rodolfo Jacobo

Foreword

The epigraph to this important pilot project aptly highlights the importance of the Bracero Program that began as part of the war effort in World War II: "One of the most vital links" of that effort, it reminds us, "was agricultural production"(21). The *braceros* are important personae of that great generation that struggled valiantly on so many fronts to preserve democracy from the Axis threat. And just as more than a thousand United States veterans of WWII are estimated to be dying daily, so too are the original *braceros* of those important war years beginning to disappear from among us. The urgency now felt about recording and transcribing interviews with surviving United States veterans of the war must be inclusive too of these other veterans who were driven into the United States by the geopolitics of hunger and by the desire to improve their lot and those of their families. Their stories too, extending to1964—well beyond the end of WW II in 1945—must be preserved,…and in their own words. Manuel García y Griego, in his seminal study "Strangers in Our Fields," reports that Ernesto Galarza "reproduc[ed] interviews held with *braceros* in and out of work camps in California." *Los Braceros: Memories of Bracero Workers 1942-1964*, a compilation of translated, structured oral interviews, continues in that tradition.

This project further highlights the need for the gathering and preservation of more structured as well as open-ended oral interviews, whose publication will include further documentation and analysis. The preservation of existing documents, testimony, family correspondence, photos, and narratives will be an invaluable research resource for future studies. Hence, the significance of *Los Braceros: Memories of Bracero Workers 1942-1964* transcends the anecdotal; it is a study of the continuing, cyclic push-pull pattern of migration *al norte* that antedates the *bracero* program and that continues to this day.

This book is, furthermore, uncannily timely (2004), as we see President George W. Bush, on the eve of the presidential primaries, present a revival of a "Guest Worker Plan" to dry out some eight to eleven million undocumented immigrants living in the United States. We see, that however it is accomplished, a supply of cheap Mexican labor will be made available to American business. United States Government, labor, and business have historically been the power players, with the Mexican Government ritually accommodating itself to the dynamics of the United States labor market and to the United States Government's accommodation to the needs of American big business. Mexican laborers are the commodity in silent expectation of improving life-chances for themselves and especially for their families. It is in this same vein that League of United Latin-American Citizens (LULAC) President Hector Flores recently stated: "Temporary guest worker programs have a history of abuse and their expansion leaves workers vulnerable to further inequities" (Gabriela D. Lemus, LULAC, 12/16/03).

Again, the recycling of the Bracero Program (1942-64) is being seen as a remedy/substitute for undocumented entries to the United States, under color of law. This, with the unspoken understanding of mass deportations to follow someday, Operation Wetback[1] (1954-55)—for fear of alleged "subversive

---

[1] 1954 Operation Wetback: United States Immigration arrests and deports close to four million workers of Mexican decent, many of them American nationals. They are seen as an economic problem.

and Communist infiltration," now read "terrorists." Politicians can, therefore, at once accommodate the demands of powerful business interests that support their candidacies, as well as the xenophobia of those fearing a de facto re-conquest, especially of the Southwest, by Mexican immigrants. In any case, the employers of undocumented workers need not fear reprisals, and cheap Mexican labor will, somehow, always be available because of their hunger and their search for a better life, as we see in these powerful personal accounts.

The process that these men went though in getting to a job as a *bracero*, as described by García y Griego, included six stages. Their contracts would bring them into the United States for short periods or sometimes for consecutive contracts, after which they would have to repeat the process, with some priority, however, because of their having successfully completed a contract. These steps included the following:

1. In the interior of Mexico, the men first had to be accepted by representatives of the Mexican government as candidates for becoming a *bracero*.

2. Representatives of the US Department of Labor, at recruiting points, initially in the interior of Mexico, "acting as agents [of prospective American employers], selected men they thought fit for agricultural work." Stories are told of men roughing up their hands, rubbing them on cement to develop calluses so that they would be chosen. Urbanized Mexicans, unused to hard manual labor, even if they got a contract, often could not endure the demanding work of stoop labor and the torments of the short hoe, now outlawed thanks to the efforst of César Estrada Chávez and his United Farm Workers' Union.

3. Immigration and Naturalization personnel fingerprinted and documented the men, also initially in the interior of Mexico.

4. "Candidates were transported to US contracting centers at the border." Accounts tell of men being crowded like cattle into boxcars, with a barrel of water dangerously sloshing about, and of interminable hours of travel without adequate food and sanitation facilities. "It was terrible, and we were tired and becoming desperate. It felt as though we would never arrive. There were people from everywhere in Mexico—from Oaxaca, Jalisco, Guanajuato and Michoacán. Some of them were indigenous peoples" (José Luis Gutiérrez-Navarro). Often, upon arrival and screening, they were sent out to work immediately.

5. Many of these accounts speak bitterly of humiliating treatment while being screened by US Public Health, everyone being sprayed with delousing powder like common animals. "The powder was very strong. The powder used was like the one used to disinfect or kill some sort of plague...We were offended because we felt that they saw us as inferior. At least, we felt that way" (Rodolfo Jacobo-Páramo).

6. The survivors of this gauntlet "were left to be considered by visiting employers and their agents."

These men pursued the dream of a better life, the hope of something somehow better. They had to be careful when forming small mutual-aid groups among themselves to help one another in their struggle to survive in a foreign land. They were ready to endure untold hardships and dangerous working conditions; they were willing to labor long hours even when injured and with little or no medical recourse except what they could improvise among themselves. As one reader of these accounts was moved to say, " No one should be treated that way—*bracero*, documented or undocumented person—no one should be treated that way!"

Too often, they had no choice but to endure arrogance, abuse, and humiliation because they were desperate for work. "But we came," Rodolfo Jacobo-Páramo tells us, "with the desire to work, so we did what we were told. That was how it was." They wanted to return home with something to show for their efforts. Young and old, their self-deprecating understanding became one of acceptance: "*vamos a sufrir, porque así la tenemos sentenciada—* let's go and suffer because that is our lot." So much, as they saw it, depended on *la suerte* "luck." If they had a special skill, had a good boss, or their work caught his attention, they were sometimes rehired without having to return to Mexico. They might even hit the jackpot and the boss might help them get a Green Card with which they could later bring their family into the land of opportunity.

The dynamics of this process exploited a needy labor force to the benefit of capital while helping Mexico to bring dollars into its economy. Expatriate workers continue to be an escape valve for the failure of Mexico's land reform programs of the Revolution of 1910. This emigration brought relief to Mexico's rural economy and to the urban explosion that followed. Mexicans in the United States became bridges to their homeland and ports of entry for those who were to follow. In their struggle to survive in the United States, I vividly recall how in the '30s, as the United States came out of the depression and into WWII, my parents and the Mexican community in Los Angeles would speak with such respect and expectation of *el consul mexicano*.[2] They saw the Mexican consul as a defender of their human rights in what was often a hostile environment, even as they were studying to become naturalized American citizens.

Today, we see the survivors of those braceros rallying to recover million of dollars in missing wages. The agreement of August 4, 1942, stipulated that "agencies of the Government of the United States [would] be responsible for the safekeeping of the

---

[2] The mexican consul.

sums contributed by the Mexican workers toward the formation of their Rural Savings Fund" transferred to Wells Fargo Bank for the account of the Bank of Mexico, to be transferred to the Mexican Agricultural Credit Bank, which would in turn "assume responsibility for the deposit, for the safekeeping and for the application, or in the absence of these, for the return of such amounts." This money has not been seen to date. The Mexican Government is looking into the matter.

These stories are ever ancient, ever new—stories of the will of the human spirit to survive in the face of adversity. The stories that follow give a heart and a face to the facile stereotypes generalized about Mexicans and Mexican Americans, and those of us who call ourselves Chicanos, who are proud to come from such parents with such a will to struggle to survive and to be, to create that something more. This has been the tale of countless generations of immigrants who continue to come to make this country what it is today.

César A. González-T. (Prof. Emeritus)
Founding Chair, Chicano Studies Department
San Diego Mesa College

Table of Contents

José Rodolfo Jacobo

Timeline

Economics and Politics of Mexican Immigration to the United States

Late 1800s
The latter part of the 19th century saw changes of a social, political and economic nature that would cement the path for the Bracero Program.

1876 **Porfirio Díaz Dictatorship Begins**
In the 34-year Díaz rule over Mexico, several projects were initiated that created and cemented the dependence between Mexican Labor and American Business. These included an expansion of the railroad—generally northward; a shift in the country's focus from agriculture to industry; increased concentration of land ownership; consolidation of a debt peonage system/tienda de raya; an estimated 57% decline in real income; US investments increased, leading to the control of 75% of all mineral holdings in Mexico; growth of border cities; an increase in foreign investments, leading to the control of 76% of all corporations, 95% of mining, 89% of industry, 100% of oil, 96% of agricultural production; the Mexican economy found itself in a state of underdevelopment and dependence on US and foreign economic interests.

1882 **Chinese Exclusion Act**
Creates labor shortage in United States.

1885 **Alien Contract Labor Law**
Prohibits recruiting and importation of contract labor.

1887 **Dingley Tariff**
Import tariff on sugar motivates the creation of the sugar industry in the United States. It also creates a demand for cheap labor in and outside of the Southwest.

José Rodolfo Jacobo

Push/Pull Factors: 1900-1930
Political, social, and economic conditions in Mexico and in the United States cause displacement and motivate immigration.

1902 **Land Reclamation Act**
      Augments the growth of specialized farming, agricultural expansion, and increased demand for labor.

1907 **Gentlemen's Act**
      Restrictions on Japanese immigrants created a labor shortage.

1909 **Cotton Value**
      California—$12,000; Arizona—$730

1910 **The Mexican Revolution Begins**
      The Mexican Revolution continued for eleven years. During this time Mexico was in a state of fluctuation. With the end of debt peonage system, there is economic dislocation, with attendant political consequences; some of the refugee population begins to flee to the U.S. These factors create a depressed Mexican economy and a lower standard of living.

1917 **Immigration Law**
      Aimed primarily at Eastern Europeans, the law imposed a literacy test—must read in at least one language; imposed a head tax of $8. Agriculture, mining, and transportation industries lobby for the exclusion of these restrictions on Mexican immigration. Mexicans were exempt from the literacy test and head tax until 1921.

1919 **Cotton Value**
      Cotton Industry peaks; demand for labor is high. California— $9 million; Arizona—$20 million.

1921 **Immigration Act**
      Quota law—limits on immigration based on numbers already in U.S. Economic interests seek exemption for Mexico.

1924 **Immigration Act**
      Also known as the Johnson Bill—further restricts Southern and Eastern European immigration; places quota on Asian immigration.

1926 **Congressional Debate**
      Box Bill—establishes quota provision on entire Western European Hemisphere; restrictive quota on Mexico only. Both bills defeated due to lobbying by southwestern economic interests—mining, transportation, agriculture.

1930   **Harris Bill**
Would reduce Mexican immigration from 58,000 to 1,900; rationale includes unemployment and un-Americanism. Great Depression ends debate; U.S. initiates the Repatriation Program of the 1930s.

1930   **Repatriation Program**
The Hoover Administration deports over half a million Mexicans, many of them American citizens, to Mexico blaming them for the nations economic problems.

The Bracero Program: 1942-Present

The Bracero Program begins as a wartime measure to supply the United States labor. The program did not "officially" end until well after the end of the war...or has it?

1954   **Operation Wetback**
United States Immigration arrests and deports close to four million workers of Mexican decent, many of them American nationals.

1964   **The Bracero Program Officially Ends**
It is estimated that as many as five million Mexican men took part in this program.

1986   **Amnesty Program**
Reagan Administration gives general amnesty to undocumented immigrants with the hope of securing that labor force.

1994   **Operation Gatekeeper**
American policy attempting to shut down the main points of undocumented entry into the United States. The policy includes using dangerous terrain as natural barriers. More than two-thousand people have lost their lives attempting to cross the border since these operations began.

1994   **Proposition 187**
Would deny education and healthcare to the undocumented, affecting children in particular.

2004   **Proposed Guest Worker Program**
Controversial plan to create a Guest Worker Program. The legacy of the exploitation and the violation of agreements of the earlier program overshadows such a proposal.

José Rodolfo Jacobo

The Bracero Program
1942-1964

*World War II placed great demands on all sectors of
society. Any weak link in the chain of aggregate action
could have proved damaging to the cause of victory...
one of the most vital links was agricultural production.*

José Rodolfo Jacobo

$\mathcal{T}$he Bracero Program, as it became known, began as demands for labor increased in the United States once the country had been catapulted into World War II. The demand was especially high in the agricultural industry.[1] Faced with a labor shortage, farmers quickly turned towards Mexico, demonstrating a continuing pattern of dependency on Mexican labor by agribusiness and other sectors in the United States that had existed prior to the war. Referring to California between 1900 and 1942, Doctor Ernesto Galarza wrote, "It was in this period that the California farmers and the Mexican poor discovered one another."

Unquestionably, it was then that Mexican labor became the labor of choice for agribusiness, replacing Chinese, Japanese and Filipino workers in the American agricultural fields. Writing about the reliance on Mexican labor by the American agricultural industry, Galarza noted: "Until the machines should become clever enough to tell the difference between ripe peaches and green ones, and to pick and sort without bruising them, human arms and fingers would remain indispensable."[2]

World War II took this dependency on Mexican labor by agribusiness and other sectors to an even higher level. According to Richard B. Craig, "World War II placed great demands on all sectors of society. Any weak link in the chain of aggregate action could have proved damaging to the cause of victory." He goes on to state, "One of the most vital links was agricultural production."[3] As the war progressed, American farmers were asked to increase their production, a task that proved difficult to complete without an adequate supply of labor.

---

[1] The American support of England had already created a demand for labor before the United States even entered the war.

[2] Ernesto Galarza, *Merchants of Labor: The Mexican Bracero Story* (Santa Barbara: McNally & Loftin Press, 1964) 14.

[3] Richard B. Craig, *The Bracero Program: Interest Groups and Foreign Policy* (Austin: U of Texas P, 1971) 39.

Given a window of opportunity, farmers were soon demanding imported labor as a matter of necessity for national defense. Recognizing the controversial proposal, Secretary of Agriculture Claude Wickard secretly traveled to Mexico City "to address an inter-American conference on agriculture, but actually to initiate negotiations with the Mexican government on importation of Mexican farm workers."[4]

Wickard returned to the United States, having successfully received the approval of the Mexican government, and in May 1942, preliminary discussions were held with the Mexican Embassy in Washington DC. At this meeting, the Mexican government presented its terms for such a program of imported labor. In particular, the Mexican government sought a bi-lateral international commission that should administer the program. This would insure that both sides would be able to implement and regulate the program. The Mexican government sought to have a strong position in the discussions of the program in order to be able to address issues of importance to Mexican authorities —issues such as racial discrimination, payment of repatriation costs, the assurance that migrants would not be encouraged to remain in the United States, and proof that the need for Mexican labor truly existed.[5]

The preliminary discussions served to pave the way for the signing of the first international executive agreement and to clarify the guidelines on the issues. The agreement was ratified in Mexico City on August 4, 1942, two months after the Republic of Mexico had declared war on the Axis Powers.[6] The program lasted well beyond the end of World War II, which ended with the surrender of Japan on August 14, 1945. For the following twenty-

---

[4] *Atlantic Coast Farm Workers and the Fruits of Their Labor: Making of Migrant Poverty, 1870-1945* (U of North Carolina P, 1997) 167-68.
[5] Galarza, 47.
[6] Galarza, 47.

two years, some five million Mexican men would be legally contracted to work on United States farms under the Mexican Labor Program, or Bracero Program, as it is commonly known.

Between 1942 and 1951, Mexican workers were admitted to the United States as temporary workers under various governmental authorities that included the War Man-Power Commission. Throughout its 22-year existence, the program would experience numerous changes. The provisions of the program under the 1942 Executive Agreement which to some extent served as the foundation for future agreements, many of which led to strain relations between both countries, were as follows:

1. It is understood that Mexicans contracted to work in the United States shall not be engaged in any military service.
2. Mexicans entering the United States as a result of this understanding shall not suffer discriminatory acts of any kind in accordance with the Executive Order No. 8802 issued at the White House June 25, 1941.
3. Mexicans entering the United States under this understanding shall enjoy the guarantees of transportation, living expenses, and repatriation established in Article 29 of the Mexican Labor Law.
4. Mexicans entering the United States under this understanding shall not be employed to displace other workers, or for the purpose of reducing rates of pay previously established.

To implement the general principles mentioned above, specific clauses were established. These included:

Contracts:
a. Contracts will be made between the employer and the worker under the supervision of the Mexican government. (Contracts must be written in Spanish.)

b. The employer (Farm Security Administration) shall enter into a contract with the sub-employer, with a view to proper observance of the principles embodied in this understanding.

Admission:

The Mexican health authorities will, at the place whence the worker comes, see that he meets the necessary physical conditions.

Transportation:

a. All transportation and living expenses from the place of origin to destination, and return, as well as expenses incurred in the fulfillment of any requirements of a migratory nature shall be met by the employer.

b. Personal belongings of the workers, up to a maximum of 35 kilos per person, shall be transported at the expense of the employer.

c. In accord with the intent of Article 29 of the Mexican Federal Labor Law, it is expected that the employer will collect all or part of the cost accruing (a) and (b) of transportation from the sub-employer.

Wages and Employment:

a1. Wages to be paid to the worker shall be the same as those paid for similar work to other agricultural laborers in the respective regions of destination; but in no case shall this wage be less than 30 cents per hour (U.S. currency); piece rates shall be so set as to enable the worker of average ability to earn the prevailing wage.

a2. On the basis of prior authorization from the Mexican Government, salaries lower than those established in the previous clause may be paid those emigrants admitted into the United States as members of the family of the worker under contract and who, when they are in the field, are able to become agricultural laborers, but who, by their condition of age or sex, cannot carry out the average amount of ordinary work.

b. The worker shall be exclusively employed as an agricultural laborer for which he has been engaged; any change from such type of employment shall be made with the express approval of the worker and with the authority of the Mexican Government.

c. There shall be considered illegal any collection by reason of commission or for any other concept demanded of the workers.

d. Work for minors under 14 years shall be strictly prohibited and they shall have the same schooling opportunities as those enjoyed by children of other agricultural laborers.

e. Workers domiciled in the migratory labor camps or at any other place of employment under this understanding shall be free to obtain articles for their personal consumption, or that of their families, wherever it is most convenient for them.

f. Housing conditions, sanitary, and medical services enjoyed by workers admitted under this understanding shall be identical to those enjoyed by the other agricultural workers in the same localities.

g. Workers admitted under this understanding shall enjoy as regards occupational diseases and accidents the same guarantees enjoyed by other agricultural workers under United States legislation.

h. Groups of workers admitted under this understanding shall elect their own representatives to deal with the employer, but it is understood that all such representatives shall be working members of the group. The Mexican consuls in their respective jurisdiction shall make every effort to extend all possible protection to all these workers on any questions affecting them.

i. For such time as they are unemployed under a period equal to 75 percent of the period (exclusive of Sundays) for which the workers have been contracted they shall receive a subsistence allowance at the rate of $3.00 per day. For the remaining 25 percent of the period for which the workers have been contracted during with the workers may be unemployed they shall receive subsistence on the same basis that are established for farm laborers in the United States. Should the cost of living rise this will be a matter for reconsideration. The master contracts for workers submitted to the Mexican Government shall contain definite provisions for computation of subsistence and payments under this understanding.

Saving Fund:
The respective agency of the Government of the United States shall be responsible for the safekeeping of the sums contributed by the Mexican workers toward the formation of their Rural Savings Fund, until such sums are transferred to the Mexican Agricultural Credit Bank, which shall assume responsibilities for the deposit, for their safekeeping and for the application, or, in the absence of these, for their return.

Numbers:
As it is impossible to determine at this time the number of workers who may be needed in the United States for agricultural labor employment, the employer shall advise the Mexican Government from time to time as to the number needed. The Government of Mexico shall determine in each case the number of workers who may leave the country without detriment to its national economy.[7]

---

[7] John Chala Elac, *The Employment of Mexican Workers in US Agriculture, 1900-1960: A Binational Economic Analysis* (Los Angeles: U of California P, 1961).

The Program did not go unchallenged and, in fact, faced bitter opposition both in the United States and in Mexico. In the United States, unions were particularly against the program. Labor unions, including the AFL-CIO and its agricultural workers union, the Agricultural Workers Organizing Committee, opposed the importation of Mexican labor. Unions claimed that there existed no shortage of labor in the United States and charged growers with paying such low wages that only foreign labor would be attracted to such industries. In other words, "there was no shortage of workers, only a shortage of wages."[8]

Human rights organizations, as well as church councils, joined the unions in their open rejection of the Bracero Program, citing numerous social issues. Unions and church councils charged farmers with racism, as some American farmers made claims that Mexican labor possessed an inherent physical ability and stamina that domestic workers simply did not have. This proved to be ironic since many of the displaced domestic American agricultural workers were of Mexican descent. Both unions and church groups came across as protective of the *bracero* and accused agribusiness not only of racial discrimination, but also of underpayment and exorbitant prices at company stores. Unions in particular were interested in protecting their members who faced competition from the inexpensive and unorganized labor from the south. While farmers claimed the imported Mexican labor had no effect on American wages and benefits, the unions claimed (and could prove) otherwise.

In Mexico, the Catholic Church opposed the Bracero Program for several reasons, including the disruption of family life and thus, the obliteration of the Mexican family. Other concerns of the Catholic Church included the "supposedly immoral life led

---

[8] Craig, 28.

by the migrant during his stay" in the United States and "contact with such allegedly ubiquitous phenomena as prostitution, alcohol and gambling." All of this was clearly influenced by the anti-Protestantism of the Catholic Church. The fears of the Catholic Church were not exclusive to the Mexican Catholic authorities; by 1953, the Vatican requested that Mexican priests accompany the migrants for the purpose of providing "secular and spiritual aid."[9]

Opposition to the exodus of Mexican labor, however, found more substantial grounds in the economic and political arenas. It was feared that the Mexican economic structure would itself suffer the loss of tens of thousands of skilled laborers. In particular, industrialists who needed skilled labor feared this. The National Farmers Confederation, one of the country's most powerful unions, questioned the impact on the harvesting and cultivation of the Mexican crop as well as unfair competition by the United States farmers. The argument was that Mexican labor allowed for a surplus of American cotton, which when dumped on the world market undermined the Mexican cotton industry.[10] The most powerful economic argument, however, was that the Bracero Program "fostered an even greater economic dependency of the United States."[11]

Politically, the Mexican authorities adopted a pro forma attitude, alarmed only by the desertion of Mexican farmers of their own private plots. Other *politicos*, especially those on the political "left," saw the Bracero Program as almost demeaning and shameful. In the words of Richard B. Craig, the program was "nothing less than a conscience gall."[12] The position was based on the perception of the left that Mexicans were not only desired

---

[9] Craig, 28.
[10] Craig, 21.
[11] Craig, 21.
[12] Craig, 22.

as cheap exploitable labor, but also faced racial and religious discrimination in the United States. To the Mexican "left," the Bracero Program was yet one more classic example of economic imperialism. It was a classic example of gringo capitalist colonial exploitation of Mexican labor and of Mexico itself.

The opposition, however, was not strong enough to deter the passage and the existence of the program. In the United States, the powerful agricultural lobby succeeded in the passage of the program, which lasted for twenty-two years, surviving political and economic challenges. In fact, it may be argued that the greatest dangers that the Bracero Program faced came from the Mexican government itself. Challenges resulted in numerous changes to the initial agreement of 1942, including the passage of Public Law 78 in 1951. This law was passed at the insistence of the Mexican government as it attempted to regain control over the hiring of Mexican workers, which, from April 1947 to August 11, 1951 had been based on contracts between workers and employers.[13]

In Mexico, despite the fears of the Catholic Church and the Mexican "left" (which, ironically, found themselves on the same side of an argument, although for entirely different reasons) the Mexican government entered into the Bracero Program. The reasons, one may conclude, were primarily based on economic grounds. It was estimated that between 22 and 120 million dollars entered Mexico annually from Mexican farm workers. The infusion of such amounts into the Mexican economy must have been a factor in the decision of the Mexican government to enter into the Bracero Program.

While several studies exist on the Bracero Program, there is little on the actual memories of the *braceros* themselves, outside of a study by Dr. Ernesto Galarza. This being the case, a great

---

[13] Elac, 44.

and important part of American history is being lost in the crevices of historical research. Some scholars suggest that the Bracero Program "established the contours of modern Mexican immigration flows and gave rise to the social, political and cultural issues that dominate the discourse over immigration in the present."[14]

Richard Griswold del Castillo notes that many of these men who stayed behind, settled and later brought their families, and influenced the development of barrios and colonias in the United States. With time their children, Mexican Americans and Chicanos, became the expanding Mexican-heritage population of the United States.

What follows are some examples of personal testimonies of Mexican men who came to the United States as *braceros* between 1942 and 1964. An attempt has been made to offer a selection that will show, first, the reasons why Mexican men joined the Bracero Program, and second, their experiences as *braceros*. Please note that in the translation process we have tried to be as accurate as possible. Nevertheless, the problems of translation may be present in these stories, including the translation of dialect and regionalisms.

---

[14] David Gutiérrez, *Between Two Worlds: Mexican Immigrants in the United States* (Wilmington: Scholarly Resources Inc, 1996).

José Rodolfo Jacobo

hen we heard that they were contracting workers to go to the United States, we all wanted to go. I could not go, however, because I was a soldier in the Mexican Army. I was the chauffer of a general by the name of Anacleto López. But I really needed to go because I had a son that was ill, and I needed the money for his surgery. So I asked the general for permission. I asked him to allow me to go. Laughing, he said, "Sure, go and try your luck." And so I went.

The year was 1942. The United States was at war and needed labor from Mexico. The Mexican government and the Americans entered into an agreement that same year that would let Mexican men work in the United States. And as I said before, when we heard that they were contracting workers to go to the United States, we all wanted to go. We saw it as an opportunity to make good money. Once I had been given permission by my commanding officer, my *compadre*,[1] José Manuel Sandoval and I went to the stadium in Mexico City, which had been designated as the contracting center.

The stadium was filled with hundreds of men, all looking for the same chance to go as *braceros* to the United States and make some money to help their families. Men from all over the country were there, most of them poor. We were all crowded in the stadium; and suddenly, there in the middle of the crowd, we found ourselves being sprayed with hoses in order to stop, as I later found out, an infestation of lice. Boy, they gave us quite a shower.

The next morning the man in charge of the contracts—his name was Guillermo—came by and I explained my situation. I told him I needed to go to the United States because of the illness in my family. He told me to go ahead and go to the United States

---

[1] Godfather of one's child or father of one's godchild; in Mexican culture this is a very strong bond. Becoming *compadres* shows great mutual trust, since the godfather accepts responsibility for the child's well-being if the parent were to die.

and that, once I was there, to write him and he would send my son to Mexico so that he could receive medical attention. And so that happened and we soon found ourselves on our way to the United States.

When we crossed the border at Ciudad Juárez to El Paso, Texas, our hearts pounded wildly, *mi 'ja*.[2] We were afraid because we were in a totally strange country, and I was also worried because I had never really done any other kind of work but mine. I had always been a chauffeur. When we were on the United States side, they took José Manuel and me to Riverside, California, near Colton.

It was a very long way from Ciudad Juárez to California. During the trip, we entertained ourselves by counting the wagons on the trains that were going by with military equipment and personnel on their way to Europe. Sometimes the soldiers would wave at us and we waved back. The trains passed really close to each other, and sometimes the American soldiers would even give us a cigarette.

Colton was the location for the base of an American military squadron, but the squadron was not there. The men had been shipped out to Europe to fight in the Second World War and we were housed there. It was nice and clean there, and we even had a Catholic priest. He saw that most of us were Catholic and he started to build a small shrine so that we could attend Mass on Sundays.

Not everyone went to Mass, however. On Sundays, five buses would also arrive to take us to town to the movies or to drink wine. There was a lot of drinking and, sometimes, even fancy women would come to take money from the *braceros* and things would get very wild. But that was only on the weekends, because during the week it was all work.[3]

---

[2] *Mi 'ja* is a term of endearment. His granddaughter Rose Conde was the interviewer.
[3] Don Jesús laughs at the memories.

Buses arrived early in the day to take us to work. There were about twenty of us per bus. They would take us to several groves to pick oranges. There, we had to put one ladder on top of the other to reach one or two oranges that were way on top of the trees. Sometimes, however, they would take us to Japanese groves and there the trees were really short, but falling over full of oranges. We were given cutters to cut the oranges; but some, in order to go faster, would just pull the fruit from the tree. I did everything as I was told, and it helped me get along with my boss, and so I soon became a driver. That was a lot easier, and I even, had a helper.

We worked in the United States for two years of the war. The end of our contract came in 1944, and Rogelio tried to convince me to go to Canada. Work was good there he said. But I had completed my contract and my son had already received the surgery he needed, so I decided to go back to Mexico. If I had wanted to stay, I could have stayed in the United States. The bosses there wanted me to stay because I was also a good mechanic.

Nevertheless, I had made my decision. I was worried about my son and wanted to go home. In fact, when I was in Mexico I received a bonus check and a letter, from the company where I was working, asking me to come back to the United States. But I was home and back to my military job. Rogelio went to Canada. When we parted, he gave me a gift—a wallet with ten dollars inside—so that I would always remember him, he said.

Boy, I remember how the trip to the border seemed endless. The train did not seem to go as fast as when they brought us into the United States. That's the way it always seems when one is coming home. We had some hard times, but we had to better ourselves. What could we do? But I had no desire to go back. That was my luck. I chose my way.[4]

---

[4] Don Jesús grows tired and the interview comes to an end. He died later that year.

Espiririón Salazar.
1920

We needed work, and the Americans needed our labor.

José Rodolfo Jacobo

My name is Espririón Salazar. I am from a small village called El Refugio near the town of San Francisco del Rincón. It is in the state of Guanajuato. The village was very small, and we had to go to San Francisco del Rincón if we needed anything at home. I must have been fifteen years old the first time I came to the United States back in the early 1920s. We were farmers and dedicated our lives to working in agriculture growing *maíz*.[1] We were so poor that we did not own land other than the land our house sat on.

We worked, like so many others, for the haciendas, which were still in existence in many parts of Mexico. Many of the hacienda workers lived in the housing that the hacienda had for the workers, but we had a separate place. That hacienda called *La Cañada del Negro* was a place where many of us worked to make ends meet. I started working for them when I was ten. Many, many people worked there from our village and other villages. The hacienda had its year-round workers but we were seasonal and temporary workers. Sometimes we all worked for a day, other times much longer. But it was not like the old haciendas, where we had to work by force and the work was hard.

There at *La Cañada del Negro* we planted and harvested, as well as prepared the fields for the corn and made irrigation ditches. Sometimes we dug great big water holes, all by hand. Most of the time, we worked up to ten hours a day. It was hard work, but not like before when my father and grandfather worked in the old haciendas. I remember my pay, as a youngster, was six cents a day and a set amount of corn. The wage for the older workers was twenty-five cents a day and their part of corn. That was our wages. To make ends meet then, we would also cultivate wheat with others. Usually, someone would let us borrow part of their land if we worked, and later gave them half of the harvest. That was very common in Mexico at the time.

---

[1] Corn.

That is why, when the opportunity came to come specially contracted to the United States, as in the Second World War, I came like so many others. We heard of the opportunity through others who had already come to the United States. That was always the case. Someone would go and come back with some money and would make the rest of dream of similar success. And so we started coming across the border. Not all of us did; those who could make a living in Mexico stayed. Others did not come for the opposite reason: they did not have the money to make the trip. It was expensive to come all the way to the border. If I remember correctly, we paid around fifty pesos for the trip to the border.

My story is typical. I was lured by the fact that I saw that those who came to work in the United States returned with a little money and clothing. So I told my parents that I too wanted to go to the United States. With great sadness, they accepted my decision, knowing how difficult things were at home. And so I came for most of my life, since 1920, to work in the United States. Now I am just here to visit. I am too old to work now; I cannot work anymore.

There were so many of us who came. All who could and all who needed came to work in the United States. Such was our need. It was simply difficult to make a living in Mexico. Many of us came for a few contracts and then went back home. Others stayed much longer, as long as they could. Our contracts were done in the city of Guanajuato. The train brought us from Guanajuato to the border. In my case, I came through Ciudad Juárez, but I eventually ended up in Santa Paula, California, picking lemons. The work was difficult, but over all, I felt well. I was young and full of energy. I must have done a good job because I always found work with the same company and the same foremen.

One time we were contracted and were taken to Texas to work on the cotton. But, unfortunately for us, the cotton was bad and we were quickly without a job. That was one of the difficult times because we did not make enough money even to get back. I don't recall exactly where I was contracted that time, however. It must have been in Ciudad Juárez. That was the only really difficult time we had. By and large, the experience was good because we worked hard and did not give the foremen a reason to yell at us. We worked and would not talk so as not to get in trouble.

Some foremen were real *coyotes*.[2] They would hide in the trees to see if we did our work and if we were working fast and doing it right. Some men were fired simply for talking. The foremen fired many just for talking, saying, "go talk in your own country." It also depended on how we were getting paid, if by the hour or by the day, or even by piecework. We usually worked six days a week, resting on Sundays. We spent Sundays in the barracks talking to our friends. We usually made good meals on Sundays and felt at home. They were difficult times; but when you are young and the need is such, borders are the last things you worry about. We needed work and the Americans needed our labor.

---

[2] In this case, the term coyote refers to the foremen being vigilant of the workers.

Marcelo Zepeda

1945

How far am I from the land I've been born in; immense nostalgia invades my thought.

José Rodolfo Jacobo

I was born in Panuco, a small village in the state of Sinaloa. My father's name was Macedonio Zepeda Hernández and my mother's name was Clarita Orona Morales. They had five children, four boys and a little girl. I was the youngest of the five. I was born on October 7, 1916. I didn't have the privilege of knowing my father because he died at the hands of evil men when I was about three months old.

My mother became a widow with five children to support. My siblings grew up in any manner they could. They grew troubled, needing a father. What little our father left us was gone very quickly because the country was at war. My mother wasn't able to give an education to my older siblings. Because I was the youngest, I was able to go to school, where I learned to read and write. But, because the resources were so scarce, I didn't study much or pursue a career either. When I was about six years old, my mom took in a little cousin of mine whose name was Lucío. He was an orphan. My mom brought him up, so I always saw him as a brother.

In my adolescence, I worked with my brothers at whatever job there was. We would harvest corn or work at the mines or at sawmills. On January 8, 1936, when I was nineteen years old, I married my wife, Paula Antonia Marín. She was seventeen years old. We recently celebrated our 65th wedding anniversary. God sent us eight children: four boys and four girls. Unfortunately, one of the girls died when she was two years old, and one of the boys died at birth in 1955. Our remaining children are Isabel, José, Susano, Victor (Lloyd), Catalina and Blanca Lucrecia.

Life in our little village was really hard, and I didn't see how we could improve. In 1945, after the loss of our second girl Tomasita—and after seeing how my family needed more food and medicines—I decided to come to the border to see if they would include me in the Braceros Contract. This was a contract arranged between the United States and Mexico because the

United States was in need of workers to come and cultivate and gather the harvest. The majority of American men were at combat during the World War II.

The process used by the Americans to hire us as *braceros* was as follows: first they will look at our hands, looking for calluses. For them, this was an indication of a hard-working man, used to tough work. After this we had a physical exam. They didn't want us to bring disease to the United States. Then, they would fumigate us as it is done with animals to destroy any microbe we had on our bodies. I was one of the fortunate ones who were hired—this is how I got to know life in the United States. I, as a lowly citizen of Mexico, never imagined that someday I would get to know the life and style of a foreign country.

I worked hard and would send a large part of my wages to my *mujercita*[1] so that she would be able to support and take care of our children and the little shack in which I had left them. Antonia has always been a good administrator. She would buy some cows and hens with what I sent, using the rest for necessities and for feeding our children.

When I finished my first contract, I was anxious to see my family. They took us in a crowded bus to the border so we could go back to our little villages. Everybody on the bus was completely silent. Some were afraid, some were in disbelief of going back to their native country. Some were acquaintances—others were strangers. All of a sudden, I thought it was a good idea to start singing a song called "Canción Mixteca"—*How far am I from the land I've been born in; immense nostalgia invades my thought.* Everybody listened to me then, and some even sang with me. When we ended the song, with tears in our eyes, we discovered that we all had a lot in common. We were anxious to touch the soil of our country and to be reunited with our loved ones.

---

[1] The little woman, a term of endearment sometimes used to describe one's wife.

As the years passed, I kept getting contracts to work as a *bracero*. It was around 1950, when my wife and I decided that we would bring the family to live in Mexicali on the California border, so I would have them closer while I worked in the United States. There in Mexicali, three of our children were born: Catalina; the boy who died, whom we called Jesús, and our youngest, Blanquita.

My wife continued with the care of our children and the administration of our home. Besides taking care of our home, she invested in a piece of land where we wanted to build our house. Some time later we started a business, a *tortilleria*.[2] The only worries I had were to support my wife regarding the children's discipline and to provide them with a father figure.

The year of 1965, I applied for emigration and to obtain my legal residency in the United States. By then, my four oldest children were not under our wing. That left only our two youngest daughters at home. Blanquita went to first grade, and Catalina started her studies at the middle school.

Because I had established a good record and was a hard working man, a job with a home was awaiting me. From 1965 to 1976, I worked tending and harvesting the date palms in the Coachella Valley, which is in southern California. My work with the date palms was reduced because I had an accident that left me with an injury that prevented me from working in the date trees.

Now, at 84, I spend my days learning to play the guitar and sometimes the accordion. I'm not a professional, but I have always loved to sing. I have appeared in public on various occasions to bring happiness to my fellow countrymen as I once did on that dark night when we *braceros* were brought to the border and to our families.

---

[1] A shop that makes and sells *tortillas*.

José Rodolfo Jacobo

My sister and brother are now no longer living, but my sweet wife, Paula Antonia, is still my support and my faithful companion since that cold night of January 8, 1936.

Audelio García

1956

They did not want to tell us she was dead. I have never felt such sadness in my life, but that is life.

José Rodolfo Jacobo

*M*y name is Audelio García. I was born on April 5, 1937. I was born in a town called Yerba Buena, in the state of Michoacán, where we lived early in my youth. My childhood, like that of so many children, was a difficult one. We had to work ever since we were children. I remember being seven years old and having to take lunch to my father and being very fearful of all the snakes. I remember we had to load and manage burros full of corn and, if we ever dropped part of a load, we would be in big trouble.

It was a hard life. In the winter, we had to get up early and walk for two hours on the icy ground to go milk the cows. I remember my *huaraches*[1] being helpless against the penetrating ice. I had to get on top of rocks to alleviate the pain that I felt. It was a hard life for a seven-year-old child. We did not go to school much since we had to work so much.

I lived in Yerba Buena, Michoacán, until I was thirteen years old, when my dad, who at the time was working in the United States, decided to move our family to the state of Nayarit. Apparently, my father had made a deal with someone for a piece of land, which, at the time, seemed promising for the future of our family. My father wrote to my mom telling her to pack all the essentials and to move. And so we did.

Unfortunately, things did not work as planned because we never got the piece of land my father thought he had secured for us. We faced great hardships. It was extremely difficult to make a living. To make ends meet, we hired ourselves out to pick cotton in the coast of Sinaloa. I also sold *agua fresca*[2] in the heat. Any kind of income would help. We were having a hard time finding a good place to call home. But when you have bad luck, you simply have bad luck. I later found out we were really close to rich farmland, which we could have had for a good price.

---

[1] Sandals.
[2] Lemonade

In Culiacán, Sinaloa, we received news that in Nayarit they were giving away free land, and so my father decided to go back to Nayarit. I remember we got to a town called Ruíz, Nayarit, and we came across a woman whose name was (or maybe is) María Medrano. She told us that in her town there was plenty of fertile land. We boarded the train again and got off in a town named Mango, about one and a half hours from Nayarit. We walked to town and the lady offered us a place to stay. I remember it was the month of May, and we ate lots of *mangos*, which were grown there at that time.

One thing we were not told, however, was of the dangerous, poisonous scorpions, which are native to the land. They were so venomous that amputation was the only way to save someone from that type of sting. About a week after we got there, a scorpion stung my brother, Arturo. Within five minutes, he was purple and we had no idea what to do. A half-hour after that he was dead. My brother's death was the first of our many tragedies. What could we do? The next day, we held the wake, and a few people came because no one really knew us.

That was the beginning of our most difficult years, which included the mental illness of my brother, Juvencio, and the death of my mother. My mother was pregnant and overworked and soon was ill. It was hard work for my mother; there was no *molino*, so she had to grind everything by hand or use a *metate*.[3] We were poor. We had beans and tortillas and not much else. And there were no doctors anywhere near our home. She grew ill and, fearing for her life, they took her to Tepic.

Three days later, I saw my brother, Rigoberto, coming home; and when we asked for our mother, he simply told us that she was coming but that she was very ill. They did not want to tell us she was dead. I have never felt such sadness in my life. But that

---

[3] A molino is a mill; a metate is a grinding stone.

is life. We held a wake again and we buried her and her baby. We carried her to the cemetery. We came home and we felt a horrible emptiness. My only consolation was that a priest who had come by earlier in the year had said that the first to die in that newly developed area would go to heaven, and it was my mother. She went to heaven.

That was not the end of our bad luck. One night the train killed fourteen of our cows. On another occasion, during a storm, lightning struck our house. God be blessed, except for some burns, all of us were unharmed; but our newborn pigs, which were under our bed, were all killed. Outside a number of animals were also killed. We were quickly going from bad to worse. We had enough to eat, but we could not do much more.

So I began to think about venturing out on my own. I desperately wanted to do something to better our situation. This is no life, I thought. I was nineteen years old and I wanted shoes and clothes; but my father was not happy about my decision and, in fact, severely opposed it. He almost became violent when I told him I had decided to go on my own: so, eventually, I ran away from home. I wanted so much to make something out of my life, and I knew no other way.

Once I had gone to Michoacán, my cousins had told me about going to *El Norte*.[4] In Mexico, I tried everything from working in the tomato harvest to cutting tobacco. But it was always difficult to make a living. So I saved as much money as I could, and when I had saved a good amount, I decided to go north. I remember getting a ride to Ciudad Obregón, in the state of Sonora. There in Ciudad Obregón, was a contracting center.

I did not know a single person in Ciudad Obregón, and had nowhere to stay; so I slept in houses that were under construc-

[4] The literal translation is "the north," but here it implies the United States. El Norte is often used to describe the United States while El Sur implies Mexico.

tion, and at night I would cover myself with newspaper. I had to wake up early and leave before the construction workers would arrive. Those were difficult days. I began to worry that my money, which I had saved, would not be enough. I was right.

As my saved money began to disappear, I decided to sell ice cream. But with my bad luck, I ended up in jail. I still do not know exactly why, but a big Yaqui Indian policeman arrested me, and I was thrown in jail. Apparently, I was selling in the wrong place. I ended up in a cell with some violent murderer, and I am sure that it was due to my mother's prayers that he did not harm me.

As soon as I got out of jail, I went to the contracting office, which they called the "control office." In that office, after you met certain prerequisites, which included picking cotton, they would send you to Empalme and from there to California to pick all kinds of crops. I signed up and it was the turn of my luck. The boss asked me where I lived, and I told him I was homeless, and he gave me shelter in his house. That night, he gave me dinner and I remember the huge flour tortillas.

Within a week I got my pass to go to Empalme, Sonora, and there I signed up. There the *gabachos*[5] would go and people would line up and get picked to work. I was picked because I was young. They brought me to El Centro and I was sent to Stockton to a town called Peterson, next to a town called Tracy. There I picked tomatoes for three months of my first contract.

---

[5] A pejorative term to refer to a foreigner of North American or European origin.

Empalme, Sonora was one of the major *bracero* contracting centers in Northern Mexico.

These tracks brought the *braceros* from their homes in Jalisco, Michoacan, Guanajuato, Oaxaca, and other states of the Mexican republic to Empalme, Sonora. These same tracks took them north to their border destinations.

Empalme, Sonora. Cargo trains such as this one transported the braceros from central Mexico to the U.S.-Mexico border. The railroad system was the lifeline of the bracero program. The travel conditions, however, were deplorable as the cargo trains were overcrowded and lacked sanitary facilities.

PROGRESSIVE GROWERS ASSN.   ES-366 # 646
SANTA CLARA: Misc. Veg. thin-hoe-harvest, $1.00 hour. Truck garden plant,
cultivate, harvest, $1.00 hr. R-syberries, pik, $1.00 hr. 90-1.00 crt.
45-50¢ 1 gal. can (#10 can). Onions top, 12¢ bushel hamper.Tomatoes ripe
load, 2½ box crew basis.
SANTA CRUZ: Misc. Veg. thin-hoe-harvest, 1.00-1.10 hour. Brussels sprouts,
hoe,-irrigate-harvest, 1.00 hour. Raspberries pik, .80-1.00/6¢ crt.
SAN MATEO: Misc. Veg. thin hoe harvest, $1.00 hr. Brussels sprouts hoe
irrigate, harvest, 1.00 hr. Dust, 1.25 hour.
SAN BENITO: Pear shaped 20½/50# box. Seed tomatoes (machine pick only)
½'20 qt. bucket. load, 2½ box crew basis.
ALAMEDA: Misc. Veg. thin hoe harvest, $1.10 hour. Lettuce weed, hoe thin
.275/45¢ crt, $1.00 hr. Harvest, 1.00 hr. 22.00 acre (thin). Cucumber
weed hoe, $1.10 hr. Harvest, 1.00 hr. 50-50 share crop basis 25½/5 gal. bucket
Tomatoes ripe load, 2½ box crew basis.
Published Scale applicable to Santa Clara, San Benito, Alameda Counties.
Tomatoes ripe pick, cannery round, .14½/50# box (321 cu.in.) 12 tons or
o er. .15½/50# box (321 cu. in.) 9 tons or over. .16½/50# box (321½ cu. in)
7 tons or over. .1¾/50# box (321½ cu. in) 5 tons or over. 20½/50# box
(321½ cu. in.) less than 5 ton. Unscheduled rates, 1st pik, 14½/50# box.
(321½ cu. in.), 2nd pick .15½/50# box (321 cu. in.) 3rd pik 20½/50# box
(321½ cu. in.)   Unscheduled rates applicable for all Counties.
 Rev.9-5-51 Sta. Clara: Cucumber pik 50-50 share.25½ gal. can.

  Rev. 9-5-51 Sta.Clara: Pizca de pepino, 50-50 arte. 25¢ gallon bote.
SANTA CLARA: Verduras en general,desahije escardar, cosecha $1.00 hora.
Troque de gardin, plantar, cultivar, cosecha, $1.00 hora. Pizca de
raspberries, 1.00 hora. .90-1.00 crt. 45-50¢/1 gal. bote (#10 bote).
Descabezar cebolla 12½'bushel cesto.Tomate maduro, cargar 2½/caja cuadrilla.
SANTA CRUZ: Verduras en general, dewahije escardar cosecha 1.00-1.10 hora.
Colecitas de bruselas escardar riegar cosecha 1.00 hora. Pizca de tas-
berries, .80-1.00/6¢ crt.
 SAN MATEO: Verduras en general, desahije escardar cosecha $1.00 hora.
Colecitas de bruselas, escardar, riegar, cosecha 1.00 hora. Ploviar
1.25 hora.
SAN BENITO: Tomate maduro, pera (shaped) 20½/50# caja. Tomate de semilla
(pizca con maquina) 6½/20 qt. bote. Cargar 2½ caja cuadrulla.
ALAMEDA: Verduras en general, desahije escardar cosecha 1.10 hora. Lechuga
desyerbar escardar desahije, .275/45¢ crt. 1.00 hora. Cosecha, 1.00 hora.
22.00 acre (desahije). Pipenos, desyerbar escardar, 1.10 hora. Cosecha
1.00 hora. 50-50 parte cuadrilla. 25½/5 gal. bote.
Escala publicar se aplica a Santa Clara, San Benito, Alameda;
Tomate maduro pizca, caneria redondo, .14½/50# caja (321½ cu. in.) 12
tonalada o mas. .15½/50# caja (321½ cu. in.) 9 tonalada o mas. 16½/50#
caja (321½ cu. in.) 7 tonalada o mas. .1¾/50# caja (321½ cu. in.) 5 tona
lada o mas. 20½/50# caja (321½ cu. in.) menos de 5 tonalada. Tarifas
sin catalago, primira pizca, 14½/50# caja. (321½ cu. in.). Secundo pizca
15½/50# caja. (321½ cu. in.) Tresera 20½/50# caja (321½ cu. in.)
/b.

Continuation of Standard Work Contract as amended. Document specifies the prevailing wages and standards of contract.

Canoga Park, Calif.
May 12, 1953

Atchison, Topeka, and Santa Fe Co.
Dear Sirs

Having worked for your Company from March to Sept of 1944 I am writing to enquire if I have any money due me, due to the recent wage increase? Or in Back Pay.

Thanking you for your trouble I remain

Asunción Jacobo Perez
7043 Alabama Ave
Canoga PARK, California

ASUNCION JACOBO PEREZ
SOCIAL SECURITY NO. 724-07-5239
Worked on the middle Division in The Track Dept.

Dear Sir
None for this term — AT&SFRRY

Letter from Asunción Jacobo to a former employer. He was inquiring about possible pending wages. The employer's response is noted by the arrow at the bottom of the page. It reads, "Dear Sir, none for this term…"

José Rodolfo Jacobo

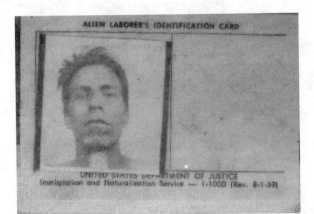

José Barajas-Chávez, Alien Labor Identification card (front and back). Wokers were required to carry these identifications at all times or risk deportation.

Bracero barracks in Holtville, CA. (Photo courtesy of Elizabeth Lopez).

Jesús Ortiz and Alejandra Simental on their wedding day, circa 1922.

Jesús Ortiz with friends in Mexico prior to entering the Bracero Program. During this time he worked as a chauffer for a general in the Mexican army.

José Jesús Jacobo-Páramo and his family in Acámbaro, Guanajuato.

Braceros who were considered to have special skills, such as this tractor driver, were able to obtain better job security and wages. (Photo courtesy of Maria Rojas.)

Hundreds of unmarked graves are testimony to the present failure of U.S.-Mexico immigration policy.

Enrique Galván
1950

Go with god.

José Rodolfo Jacobo

eft in 1950. I was doing my military service but I left regardless. I remember clearly—it was October of 1950. It was my cousin, his brother-in-law, a friend, and I. It was difficult for us. My father said to me sadly that I had to go and to "go with God." And he warned me before I left to be very careful and always be on the look out.

He told me that when we got to the big city to always ask the elderly for help. He said I could trust the elderly for directions if I needed to know where the train station was. He feared we would be exposed to violence otherwise.

We went to Guadalajara and sure enough, we got lost. But I followed my father's advice and even though a young man told me he could take us to the train station, I asked an old man for directions, and we found the train station right away.

It took us five days and nights to get from Guadalajara to Mexicali in those days because the train stopped every three to five minutes in the villages to pick up passengers. The longest it went without stopping must have been twenty minutes, and I thought to myself, "We are never going to get there." And that's the way it was the whole way.

In Sonora we went through the desert of Caborca and Puerto Peñasco. It was nothing but sand, and we were covered by it because it all came into the train. We were also covered with oil because there was oil everywhere we stepped or sat. We all looked like train engineers, full of oil and dirt and even charcoal, because in those days the trains used rocks of charcoal as fuel. It was a terrible ride, but being young we managed to survive and even see it as fun.

We finally got to Mexicali and I was shocked to see so many people there. We realized we did not know what to do or where we were going to stay. One of my companions, however, said there was a woman there from San Francisco de Rincón (where we were from) and that maybe she would give us a place to stay. She had a small restaurant called *Petra Pérez*.

We found the place and she asked where we were from. She said everybody from that ranch always ended up here and that she had too many from there now. She said that they would always leave without paying. We assured her that would pay and she finally allowed us to stay.

As we waited to see what the next step was, we went to pick cotton in Mexicali. Back then there was a lot of cotton in that area. That was in the 1950s. It was October, right when the picking of cotton is done. Three days later we decided to cross the border without any permits because we had heard that people would hire you even if you did not have contractor's identification.

I remember we walked for a couple days through the desert. There was nothing but sand everywhere. A man had told us more or less how and where to go and also to take lemons for the thirst and to never go alone.

It was the first time we crossed the desert. I remember you would be walking and suddenly sink all the way down to your knees in sand. It was a very fine kind of sand and the wind was moving it in all directions. When the winds came it moved so much sand that it even covered the *chamizales.*[1] We had to cross a canal and get to a road on the other side. Back then it was highway 80. Now it is Interstate 8 going from El Centro to Yuma.

We ran across the road and jumped on the train like those who had made the trip earlier had told us. We got off in Indio and spent the night in the cotton fields. We were afraid of getting caught by immigration. When one is here illegally any car will scare you because you think it is the Border Patrol or the police. Sure enough, we soon found ourselves surrounded by the Border Patrol, but we all got into a big icebox that was used to keep big pieces of ice. I opened it and we hid in there being careful not

---

[1] Tree shrub from the Texas-Mexico border region.

to close it or we could freeze to death. They must have known because they soon caught us.

We tried again and the third time we made it. We landed in Indio and got work picking cotton. We were going to the cotton field when the driver told us, "Boys, I got myself into a bad one. There is the Border Patrol in front of us." He could not turn back. It would have been too obvious so he took us straight to the Border Patrol. The agent quickly yelled at us to show our papers, and one by one we got off the truck and into the Border Patrol vehicle. Once again we were sent all the way to Tijuana. We tried again, and we made it once more to the same area. We went there because we knew there was work, even though it was risky. That time we worked for a few days at eight cents a pound, making enough money to buy a pair of pants before we got caught yet one more time.

That time I was asked by a man named Isaias Pérez if I dared to try it one last time and go with him. I said yes. We made it to Indio, but this time we were met by a *coyote* who asked if we wanted to go to Los Angeles. He said there was much work up there. He charged thirty dollars to get you up there, but I didn't even have thirty cents.

Rutilio González-Sánchez
1954

We were packed in a cargo train as if we were animals.

$\mathcal{My}$ name is Rutilio González-Sánchez. I am from San Juan Jaripeo, Guanajuato, in the central part of Mexico. The first year I came to the United States was in 1954, at the young age of nineteen years. I was taken to the state of Texas to pick cotton. While the work was difficult and we were far from home, I signed over and over again for the renewal of my working permit. After being in Texas for a couple of years, I was sent to work in Stockton for a while and in 1959, at the age of twenty-four, I was contracted to work in Chula Vista, California.

We came to the United States full of hopes, full of dreams. I knew that one day I would be married and have children, and I wanted money to buy a home and cattle. No one likes to leave his or her home, but we were in desperate need. We were poor people who lived from the soil. We had to leave our homes and look for opportunities; it was the best thing for us and for our families. All my mother could do was bless me. She did not know when she would see me again or even if I would return. Many never did return.

When we decided to come to the United States, we went to see a woman in Mexico City named Josefina, who was a contractor. She had what they called *listas de contratación*.[1] All we had to do was give her two turkeys and a pot of mole, and she placed us on a list.[2] She then told us we needed to be in Empalme, Sonora, near the United States and Mexican border; that was where the contracting center was located.

So we made the trip to Empalme and, sure enough, that's how it was. Once we were there, on the day the lady told us, our names were read and everyone ran to be contracted. To get contracted, however, we first had to go through a series of medical examinations. No sick people were wanted—only healthy ones to

---

[1] These were contracting signup lists.
[2] Mole is a Mexican dish.

do the work. Once we were contracted, we were sent to the border in trains. That was an awful trip that I will never forget because we were packed in a cargo train as if we were animals. Wall to wall we were packed. I remember it as if it were today.

They used to place a barrel of water in the middle of the train car so we could drink water. The barrel had no cover, and every time the train shook we would get all wet. The worst part was that the train was all wood, and so it was very humid. We endured those conditions all the way to Nogales. What could we do? When we crossed the border, we were stripped of our clothing and were sprayed with some kind of powder with high-pressure hoses. After all of that was done, the bosses came and got their workers. There they would tell us where we were going and the terms of our contracts.

The work was not too hard or at least, it felt that way because we were young, but we worked hard. Here in Chula Vista, we picked celery and tomatoes. The tomatoes we picked were the big kind. We used cutters to cut the tomato so as to make sure it would not be ruined. I still remember my boss. He was a skinny old man with a dirty cowboy hat who always used to hurry us. He was always pushing us to work faster. I used to work for a foreman named Augustín Ramírez, who we called *la ganga*[3] because he had the crew of all the fastest workers. I was fast then when I was young. I could take on anyone, but now I am old and I cannot.[4]

When I came to Chula Vista, I came with my brother, Juán, and on the weekends we used to go to Tijuana to have some fun. That was one of the nice things about working near the border back then. I have to be honest, we were not saints. We used to go looking for señoritas. Once we were in Tijuana, however, we used

---

[3] The gang.
[4] Rutilio was sixty-five years old and still working in agriculture at the time of the interview.

to go our own separate ways. We used to go to a cantina called El Burro, which I think is still there. We used to drink a beer and the girls charged ten cents for a dance. We used to also go to a restaurant called *La India María* near *La Cahuila* (Coahuila Avenue).[5] We used to meet there with our friends and my brother. One of our friends was a man named Benjamín Cortéz.

On one occasion, we all went our separate ways; and when Monday morning came, Benjamín was not at work. I told the foreman that Benjamín had not arrived, and that I was worried about him. He said, "I do not give a damn who came to work and who did not." That afternoon I took a shower, and I went to Tijuana to look for our friend. We were contracted, so we could go in and out to Tijuana. We were given a card to show the authorities. The first place I went to was to the local jail to see if he was there. I talked to the jailer who warned me that men usually gave a different name and I might not find him. Luckily, he did use his real name and I found him.

He had been arrested for disturbing the peace. I asked the jailer if I could see him, and he allowed me to. He told another officer to bring Benjamín. Benjamín was very glad to see me. He thanked me for looking for him and assured me that I was a good friend. I paid for his bail, which was 300 pesos, which was a lot of money for that time. We went back to the barracks. When the contracts were over, I embraced Benjamín, and I never saw him again. But that was the way it was when you came to this country. You make good friends with your fellow men. One could become very lonely as a bracero, and good friends were very important for company and for protection.

Once our contracts were over, if we were no longer needed, we were kicked out of the country. We had no choice but to go back home. If you were lucky, you had saved some money. If not,

---

[5] Tijuana's "red light" district.

you could be sent back home broke. No one wanted to go home without any money. That was one of the worst things that could happen to a bracero. On one occasion, we were sent home, but my brother had had some bad times and was taking no money home with him. He did not even have money for the bus, so I paid his way home.

My brother was so embarrassed about going back with nothing. I had sent money to my father to buy me a house and I got some land. My brother did not want to go home with nothing. So he asked if I would trade him a radio I had bought while I was in the United States for a piece of land. I did, and he later traded the radio for a horse and a donkey. But it was obvious that my brother had bad luck. That same year, the train killed the donkey and the horse was poisoned and died. He had no radio, no horse or donkey and no land. The bracero contract had brought him nothing but bad luck. As for me, I do not know what happened to the radio. But I still have the land, and it has given me plenty of corn. That is my story. That was my life.

José Luis Gutiérrez-Navarro
1959

At times he emptied our bags and would not pay.

José Rodolfo Jacobo

y name is José Luis Gutiérrez-Navarro; and I came from Arrandas, Jalisco. I was contracted in 1959 in Empalme, Sonora, where the contracting center was located for the *braceros*. It is far from central Mexico, near the border. I was driven from my home by poverty. I came from a large family, and it was difficult to make ends meet. I had to come north, to look for opportunity. Everyone except for my mother supported my decision to go to the United States. She was heartbroken, but accepted the fact that I had to leave because there was no other alternative. I was sad to leave my father, mother, and my brothers; but they were so poor that I had to do something. I wanted to help them. I had to leave in search of a better future.

I came with one of my brothers and a friend. My friend had a contact with the local government authorities in our town and obtained letters of recommendation for us to be contracted in Empalme. When we arrived in Empalme, it took a month and a half for our names to appear on a list to be contracted. During that time, we had to be present every morning at the contracting center in case our names were called. For six weeks, our names were not called. We were out of work and money, and we had to struggle to survive. Finally, the long awaited day arrived—the day we so desired—and our names were called.

There were so many going to work in the United States. We were on a train that was filled to capacity. There were about 1,500 men on board. I was excited to travel by train because it was my first time. I was shocked to find that there were no seats in the train and that we had to sit on the floor. We were all crowded, one on top of the other. It was terrible, and we were tired and becoming desperate. It felt as though we would never arrive. There were people from everywhere in Mexico: from Oaxaca, Jalisco, Guanajuato, and Michoacán.[1] Some of them were indigenous peoples.

---

[1] Traditionally states with a high population of immigrants.

All of us were going to work in different parts of the United States. I crossed the border through Nogales, Sonora. It was very hot there in 1959. When we finally crossed, I was taken to the small town of Glendale, Arizona, which is near Phoenix. I worked for the Melon Company, which had sites in Arizona, California, and Utah. The company had many workers. We lived in barracks, each barrack housing about 150 men. As for my job, I had to pick cotton. I remember that I was given a big bag to wrap around my waist and legs, and I was sent to pick.

I wanted to work as fast as the others, but I could not. I was too young. I tried to keep up with everyone else, but I left many unpicked plants behind. When I got to the end of the row, I was surprised to see others with a full bag, and I did not even fill a quarter. When the foreman saw me, he asked what I was doing; and I told him that I was working. He said that I was not working, that I was just walking; and that, if I wanted to earn money, I had to move my hands and work faster.

He told me that I was not going to make even enough to pay for my room and board. He was right. I was barely able to pay for my room. That, however, was only at the beginning. After a while, I became more experienced and even did extra jobs after work, such as helping out in a store. The beginning was difficult for a while. I thought I might not have a chance to make it at all. It was difficult.

Our relationship with our boss was not very good. He would always give us a hard time. We never worked fast enough for him, and he always found a reason to yell at us for picking spoiled carrots or bad cotton. At times he emptied our bags and would not pay us. We did not get along well at all. He was there to drive us hard and to get the most out of us. What made things easier for us was the many friends we made among other braceros.

Not everybody was friendly though. Some people were hard to live with. You could tell right away who was good and sincere.

You separated yourself from the others like oil and water. You needed your friends for protection and help. We helped each other when we were sick and needed medicine or money. I belonged to a group of five or six persons who got along well. We suffered together.

We worked in crews of forty or more, and at times, we worked with Filipinos and people from other countries. We felt discriminated against because we felt that they received better treatment and more tolerance than we did. They also got paid more, and we were given the worst jobs. One of the hardest jobs was to work in the fumigated fields. It hurt our skin, but we were happy to be earning money.

After working for three or four hours, our skin would break out in rashes of little red dots and we did not receive any medical attention. Sometimes they would change the crew after a week or so when it was obvious that they were allergic and getting sick. As soon as we healed, though, they sent us back to the same field. We did not have a choice. We had to work. Racism was evident, but we did not have a choice because there were no other jobs; and I was just happy to have money in my pocket.

During my second experience as a bracero, I went through the same routine including the same long train ride. I was sent to California, and I was so happy because I heard that they paid better there. I ended up in Brawley, near Calipatria, Mexicali. It was extremely hot there, reaching 115 degrees at times. I stayed there for almost a year. Then I was sent with about 1,500 braceros to El Centro, California, where I worked for a grower as an irrigator. Luckily, two people from my hometown and my Uncle Genaro, my mother's brother, were also placed there. My uncle was a hero to me because he had been a bracero for a long time and had a lot of experience. I was happy there because I made good money. I was paid fourteen cents a bag. When I received good checks, I sent money to my father in Mexico.

If I had to do it all over again, I would, but under new and better terms. When I came, contracts were never fulfilled. It was all business. When it was over, we had to go back and start all over again. It was hard to make a lot of money. I would do it now, but with better conditions in which people earn a decent wage and are treated as human beings, especially concerning health. I believe that many people have died of cancer from the pesticides we used.

There was also too much racism, which is wrong no matter how poor you are. Our government treated us like animals. Nevertheless, we ended up staying in the United States in hopes of a better life. Many of us never went back home. I eventually got my citizenship papers and, now, I am enjoying the best days of my life.[2] I thank God that my children are studying, and I hope they build a good future. My only dream now is to watch them grow.[3]

---

[2] Mr. Gutiérrez currently lives in Ventura County, California.
[3] Oscar Gutiérrez, Jr. is the interviewer. He graduated from San Diego State University with a degree in Mechanical Engineering.

José Barajas-Chávez
1957

One of the foremen saw me and, instead of offering help, he told me that I was going to have to eat the lettuce that I had bled on.

José Rodolfo Jacobo

My name is José Barajas-Chávez. I came to the United States for the first time in 1957, through Piedras Negras, Coahuila. During my first contract, I worked in Texas; but I do not recall the exact name of the small town where I was sent. Like so many others, I worked picking cotton. But while others found the transition easy, I had a difficult time in the beginning. My first contract was for a month and a half, and I barely made enough to eat and pay back what I had borrowed to make the trip to the north. When our contracts were over, the Americans took us to the border because there was no more work. They ended our contracts.

The contractors were ranchers. If they chose you, you would get in a line, and they would make you go through a series of medical exams. They would take X-rays and cover you with a powder from head to toes. If you passed all the prerequisites, then they would hire you. We would line up again and the ranchers would say how many workers they wanted—twenty, thirty— whatever he needed and for what purpose—so many workers for here and so many for there. That's the way it was done. There were a whole lot of people. On the train that I came north on, there were people from Zacatecas, Michoacán, and many other parts of Mexico. All of us ended up in different places.

In my later contracts, I ended up in Salinas, California, where I worked picking a little of everything and cleaning the tomato crop. When the tomato is small, it produces a lot of weeds. It's the same with lettuce; so it requires constant cleaning with the hoe. That type of work is backbreaking because we used a small hoe for hours and hours at a time. The long days bent over made the pain in our backs unbearable.

I was also in Los Baños, California, and in Arizona, near San Luis. In Arizona, conditions were much worse than anywhere else. We picked lettuce, which was a much more complicated process because we picked, wrapped and packed it all in the field. Some of us picked the lettuce while someone else followed, leaving boxes on the ground. Behind them came someone who packed the lettuce, and behind him, those who loaded the boxes onto the trucks.

Sometimes the workers picked the lettuce and a machine, that was right behind us, would pick it up and wrap it just as you see it in the stores. Working with the machine was much, much more difficult. We couldn't stop even to stretch our backs because, if we did, the machine would run right over us. We had to work really fast and hard to pick the lettuce. Not only did we have to be fast, but we also had to cut it in a certain way with a small knife curved at the tip in order not to damage it. We put one hand on the lettuce and, with the other hand, we cut below it with the knife. At the same time that we were cutting it, we had to pick it up so that it would be a nice clean cut.

The foremen made the work even tougher. They were really cruel and drove the people hard. It was difficult enough working fast and staying ahead of the machine without having them behind or next to us yelling for us to hurry up. On one occasion, I went to cut the lettuce and—¡en la madre![1]—I cut myself instead. I still have the scars. Blood started gushing out and one of the men working next to me told me I should get help from a white woman who was next to the machine. He told me to show her my cut and that she would give me first aid.

I went toward the machine to get medical help. They had a small first aid box in case anybody got hurt or cut himself. I was bleeding so uncontrollably that the woman I asked for help got scared and left. She just left me there and did not help me; so I wrapped my finger myself any way I could, and I went back to work. I was scared that if I didn't go back to work they would not

---

[1] Off-color remark used to express a strong emotion. Similar to "Oh shit!"

pay me. I could not afford not to be paid. I needed the money, and I also did not want to get in trouble.

When I went back to work, the pace was so fast that I could not keep my hand from bleeding; and there was blood all over the lettuce I was cutting. I could not do anything because the machine was behind me and the foreman was yelling at us that he did not want to see any *estacas*.[2] One of the foremen saw me and, instead of offering help, he told me that I was going to have to eat the lettuce that I had bled on. He ordered me to go to the truck, and all I could think of was if I was going to get paid or not. I soon was able to control the bleeding and went back to work. No one asked if I was all right. No one cared and I just wanted to work. I hid my pain.

My experience was a very sad one. One of the hardest experiences for me, however, was once when I arrived at the border in Tijuana. I had come with some men who had an uncle in Tijuana; but when we arrived, he asked who I was and he told me I had to leave, that I could not stay there because he did not know me. "Son of a bitch, " I said to myself, "what am I going to do?" I don't know the city or anyone in it. Finally, one of the men I came with, Agustín, told his uncle that he knew me and would be responsible for me. After a small discussion, I was allowed to stay. At least I had a roof over my head.

To make ends meet, I began to sell bread that one of the men from Sinaloa began to make where we lived. I had to make money to eat, so I would take a small box of bread and walk up and down the hills selling bread. I used to lose my voice yelling "bread, bread, buy bread." Sometimes I made fifty or seventy-five cents and, when things got better, I would make a dollar and fifty cents. I would then go to the store and buy *chicharrones*[3] and ten cents worth of tortillas to make tacos. I ate badly, but I had to

[2] Estacas are wooden sticks used to hold up a vine.
[3] Chicharrones are pork rinds.

91

keep some money in my pockets. It was a hard life at the border, but we all dreamed of a better life. We all had to dream to make it to the other side and work in the so desired *norte*.

Rodolfo Jacobo-Páramo

1962

We were offended because we felt they saw us as inferior.

José Rodolfo Jacobo

$\mathcal{M}$y name is Rodolfo Jacobo-Páramo. I am from the state of Guanajuaco, in the central part of Mexico. Like so many others, I came to the United States looking for opportunities. In Mexico, we lived in desperate poverty. I remember, as a child, not having enough to eat. My mother had to divide the food, including tortillas, among the children so as to be fair and to make sure we all had something to eat. My father was a farmer in Michoacán, and later, in Guanajuato. Making a living from farming in Mexico, however, was very difficult. Our land was not good land, and, if we had a dry season, or if it rained too much, our crop would be ruined and we would face desperate situations.

Things improved for us in the 1940s when my father was contracted as a *bracero*. The United States was at war and Mexican workers were needed to do different kinds of jobs, mainly agricultural work. My father was among the first *braceros* to come to the United States. He came in 1943. From that point on, we were able to make a better living because my father always had a job. Starting in 1943, my father worked all over the United States including Texas, Michigan and Arkansas. He went north year after year. He was very much a Norteño. He worked all over.

When I came of age, I followed my father's example, and I became a *bracero*. I was contracted in Empalme, Sonora, in February of 1962. The list that I signed on to was from Michoacán. My father knew the man in charge of the list, and he enlisted my brother, Jesús and me. When our time came to make the trip to the north, I was surprised at the number of people going north to work. About 2,000 of us were put on a cargo train to make the long trip from Guanajuato to Nogales, Sonora, Mexico, where the main contracting center was located.

When we arrived in Empalme, I could not believe the number of people living in the plazas and in the streets, waiting for the list and their names to be called. We were lucky and were contracted within days of our arrival. Once you were contracted, the American companies, who I suppose were associations of ranchers that solicited certain numbers of people, made arrangements to get their workers, and we were transported to the United States.

Each company seemed to have a certain number of workers they requested. There were requests for 100 or 500 people in Maricopa County with such and such company, or 100 for this or that place. For example, a large lettuce company named Interharvest contracted us, and we were brought to Phoenix, Arizona to pick lettuce. Many people crossed through Nogales; some came through Calexico. People were taken to different places to do different jobs. We came in through Nogales and were brought to Arizona to pick lettuce. All of us in Phoenix, Arizona and the whole county of Maricopa were lettuce pickers. A lot of people came to the United States in the *brazeriada*.[1]

Before crossing the border, we were given a complete checkup in Sonora. Some machines were used in case we had some sort of sickness. They threw a powder on us to disinfect everything. When we crossed over to the United States, they used more chemicals to clean us up in case some of us were sick. They again did a complete checkup on us, including our clothes. They undressed us and, once again, sprayed us with some powder as if we were some kind of *lacra*.[2] The powder gave us horrible headaches. It was very strong. The powder used was like the one used to disinfect or kill some sort of plague. I wondered why they did that. We were offended because we felt that they saw us as inferior; at least we felt that way. But we came with the desire to work, so we did what we were told. That's the thing. That is how it was.

---

[1] Brazeriada implies a large number of braceros.
[2] Lacra is a scourge, a pestilence.

I came as a *bracero* because I wanted to see the United States. I wanted to know how dollars were earned. Back home, I used to hear people talk about their contracts, and I wanted to try it myself. I had also seen how my father's trips to the north had helped our family. We came to make money, and we worked hard for it. We worked from early in the morning until it was dark, especially when the demand was high. If a company's demand for the day was not met, they would turn on the lights of the machines or cars at night so that we could complete the orders. We worked hard.

I made eighty-five cents per hour picking lettuce. Not everyone worked in the lettuce. Some people worked elsewhere. There must have been close to 5,000 people where I worked. There were twenty to twenty-five buses that took us to different places. They woke us up for breakfast at three o'clock in the morning. We did not sleep a lot. They rang a bell, and we had to get up to eat a scrambled egg and some oatmeal. The cooks were busy. From there, we got onto the buses and rode to different jobs all over.

Sometimes we went to Yuma, and we were able to sleep on the bus. We were tired, but we did not sleep much. We lived in barracks and slept in bunk beds, which made it hard. There were no private showers; sometimes about fifty of us had to shower at once. It was difficult. Although we did not sleep much and worked hard, we knew that was why we left our homeland. We came to work. It was hard, but we made friends from many places like Michoacán, Yucatán, or Palo Blanco, who shared both the good and the bad.

It was hard to leave Mexico, and I did feel sad. I left my girlfriend behind, who is now your mother [he laughs]. But that is life. I came to advance, work, and to obtain a better way of life. Many people died trying to realize that dream. Some died of illness on this side [of the border]. Some people died of sickness and some from accidents. I saw a young man from Michoacán die. He had come with the group with whom I was contracted. Some of the bodies were sent back home, but many were not. Many never went back. They died as *braceros* on the US side. Their families never saw them again.

We knew the risks. We knew it would be hard. There were dangers all over. There were also incidents of abuse in the fields. Some foremen felt superior to us and treated people badly. For example, when I worked in the lettuce thirty years ago, we used a small hoe. We were bent over to work rows that were a half to three-quarters of a mile long. It took a long time. There were huge fields of lettuce in Phoenix, Arizona, Maricopa County. Some of the foremen would yell at us to bend back down if we stopped to stretch our backs. They did not want to see anyone standing up. They said that they wanted to see us bend like staples. When we stood up straight to straighten our backs, they forced us to bend down, and we would get upset.

There was abuse. I believe that there was abuse. I remember one foreman who was a *pocho*[3] named Jesús. He treated us badly. We hated him, but we could do nothing. Nevertheless, I had wanted to go to the United States ever since I was a child. I could not go when I was younger because my father and my older brothers were going. The first chance I had though, I went. That was the last year of the contracts, which were closed then. The Bracero Program ended, but not the *braceros*. I, like so many others, stayed to work in the United States. The farmers still wanted us because we were hard workers.

---

[3] Person of Mexican descent who speaks Spanish with a great deal of English interference.

Policarpo Molina-Mendoza.

1964

El desmadre.

*M*y name is Policarpo Molina-Mendoza. I am from Santiago del Rio, Oaxaca. I came to the United States because, unfortunately, there was no work available in Mexico to make decent money. My family was poor and there was no way to make a living. I knew that they were hiring people to come to work in the United States, and I was determined to come. I struggled for three months in Mexico City, trying to get a permit. Those were difficult days because I did not know anyone in the city, and I had no money. When I finally got my permit, however, I was eager and ready to come to the United States. All the pain seemed worth it.

From Mexico City, some people were sent to Monterrey, Nuevo Leon, and others to Empalme, Sonora, in northern Mexico to the contracting centers. I was sent to the contracting center in Ciudad Juárez, across from El Paso, Texas. That was where the contracting center for that part of Mexico was located. We were contracted in the state of Chihuahua and went where we were told. Some people were sent to Yuma, others were sent to Pecos. Those who went to Chihuahua usually ended up in places like Colorado. Those who went to Sonora usually ended up in California. I ended up in Colorado in the year of 1964.

I remember being afraid. It is natural. We were coming to the United States for the first time. We were alone and didn't know anybody or anything about where we were going. Without knowing where we were going, we arrived in Ciudad Juárez in Chihuahua. We were in Ciudad Juárez for only a day before the *güeros*[1] came and loaded us into trucks to take us to Rio Vista. There, we got some food and racks to sleep on. From there I was taken to Delta, Colorado. Before we crossed the border, however, we were undressed and given medical checkups. The medical

---

[1] Güeros means the light skin ones or in this case the Americans.

exams included blood tests and x-rays. We were sprayed with chemicals too, I guess, to disinfect us.

When I came, the contracts were for only forty-five days at a time. When the contract expired, we were asked who wanted to renew their contract, and I was always the first to raise my hand. I wanted to work. After that, I got a two-month contract but was sent home because, in October, the cold weather ruined the tomato crop. I returned again because they were contracting for the state of Arizona. But on that occasion, I did not stay because a friend convinced me that in Arizona, instead of making money, we were going to lose the money we had.

I came to the United States whenever I could because, even though it was difficult, it was the only way we could feed our families. The work was very hard. When we worked with beets, we used a small hoe, and that was murder on your back. There were people who, unfortunately, could not take the pain in their waist because that was a real *friega*.[2] They called that type of work el desmadre, mainly because of the use of the small hoe, which, I think, they have gotten rid of.[3] Now they use a long hoe, but back then, we used the small one from dawn into dusk.

It was hard, but we made the best of it with our friends. One of the things I remember the most is that there were no tortillas, only bread, so we made our own tortillas. Even though our hands were all cut and full of pain, one person made the dough, another made the tortillas, and someone else cooked them. We made our lunches for the next day. Not all was bad. In some ways, I think there is more racism today than back then. Back then, if the cops stopped us, they would take us to the barracks. Today, they take you to Tijuana.

---

[2] Friega is a wasting difficult work.
[3] The "fucked up job."

Overall, my boss was a good boss. Maybe I was lucky. Maybe it was because I was a damn good worker and I was always ahead of my crew. My boss even begged me to stay when I had to leave. I could pick 200 boxes of tomatoes while the second fastest picked 125. I was paid 13 cents per box by piece-rate, which was excellent money back then because, otherwise, we got paid a dollar an hour.

But even then with eight dollars we could buy a pair of pants, a shirt, shoes, and a hat. Cigarettes cost only a quarter and sodas cost 10 cents. I worked hard. I was young, only twenty-two. Now it is all different. One of the biggest differences is the food. I almost feel like I am in Oaxaca. In the stores there are all kinds of tortillas, white and yellow, but back then, it was all white bread—only white bread.

Santiago Aguilar-Álvarez
1956

What can you possibly know about this, bracero
pendejo…go back to work.

$\mathcal{M}$y name is Santiago Aguilar-Álvarez. I was born in the town of Ameca in the state of Jalisco, but I was raised in Tuxpan, in the state of Nayarit. I was first contracted for the Bracero Program in 1956. I was anxious to better myself, to overcome my economic situation. I was not doing so badly in Mexico. I was a mechanic; but I still felt somewhat insecure about my future. In fact, I came north to the border, in part, because I had an uncle in San Luis Rio, Colorado, where I felt I had a chance at starting a new life.

Once there, however, I realized I could not make a decent living. It is difficult to live on the border, and it was much more difficult back then. Back then, like now, life on the border was a matter of survival for many. I saw some sad things that would make anyone cry, some inhumane things. I saw people without even food or water, without such things, hoping for a better tomorrow. There weren't even bathrooms. It was a terrible thing, but thank God, I did not suffer that much compared to others.

In San Luis Rio, Colorado, I ran across friends and another family member who motivated me to go to Empalme, Sonora to sign up for a contract to come and work in the United States. At first I was reluctant; I had never worked in agriculture, so I did not know what to expect, but I was willing to try new things. When you are young, things are much easier. And so, I decided to come and went through all the hardships that I am sure other companions have already shared with you.

In Empalme, the hotels were so full that people would place benches in their yards and charge a peso or two for us to sleep there. There were thousands and thousands of people in Empalme. I was lucky. I was only there for a weekend, sleeping on a bench until I went through all the medical examinations and got my documents. The medical exams bothered me because, in that moment, you were treated like an animal. Some of the exams were really degrading.

And it was not only the medical humiliation. From Emplame, we were shipped from the border to Calexico, where yet another health inspection awaited us. There we were sprayed with what I think was DDT, as if we were plants or as if they were spraying a herd of cattle. You had to go through all of that, but I was finally contracted, and I came across. Not everybody made it. Some men were rejected. Those who were sick would never make it on the final list.

In Empalme, we received our permits, but it was in Calexico where we were told where we were going to work. They called that place there in Calexico the Concentration and Repatriation Center. There, a rancher, for example, from Oregon, who needed workers would place an order, and the person in charge would tell us in very clear Spanish that they needed forty-five people in Oregon to pick this or that crop and asked who wanted to go. Not always, however, were we asked for a choice in destination.

Those who wanted to go there would raise their hands, and they would take them. Train or bus usually transported workers, but sometimes they were taken in trucks. I had been recommended by some friends to go to Arizona, and so I waited until they called for workers who wanted to pick cotton in Arizona. So that is what I did. The contracts were for a six-month period when they were for picking cotton. Once there, however, the same person contracted me three more times without my having to leave.

Unlike some *braceros*, I never had a problem. I got to work with a really nice person. John Smith was his name. He was a Senator for the state of Arizona. He was a good person. I worked with him all the time picking cotton, making three cents a pound. Depending on how fast you are, you either made good money or barely made enough to pay for your room and board, which was

---

[1] "Fucking idiot"

a dollar. I was a good worker; and I ended up with a maintenance group. It was a good job for being only twenty-three years old.

I remember a young man who was in charge of a maintenance crew that was always there. On one occasion, his GMC truck broke, and I told him I would fix it. He said "What can you possibly know about this *bracero pendejo*, go back to work."[1] I felt offended, and then he walked to go get another truck. I went and fixed the truck. I told my companions, "I am going to fix the truck even if he fires me, because I felt offended." I do not know how to pick crops, but I do know about cars. The truck was six cylinders and it was easy to fix, so I fixed it. When the foreman came back, the truck was fixed. I hid among the other workers because I thought I was going to get yelled at. A worker told him I had fixed the truck, and Mr. Smith, who was there, heard. As a result, Mr. Smith then took me and made me the tractor driver and mechanic, and I went from 60 cents to 90 cents an hour. I can call myself fortunate because of my good luck. In fact, I left, and when I came back, John Smith helped me get my green card. We became good friends. And that is how I happened to end up living here in the United States. I hope this is helpful for my children and to the future of our youth. I hope they never go through what we went through, and that they study hard. I do not want my children to go through that. We worked hard and with dignity. But it was hard.

Edmundo Ángeles Castillo
1954

*It was a good thing for the poor; I had nothing and
I thank the Lord I was able to make something in
Mexico and take care of my mother.*

José Rodolfo Jacobo

My name is Edmundo Ángeles Castillo. I am from the town of Lolotal in the state of Hidalgo. The economic conditions of my family when I was a child were extremely difficult. We lived in poverty, the kind of poverty when, sometimes, we had nothing to eat. As a child, I had to work in town ten kilometers from home. I made just twenty cents, but it was enough to help feed my family. Back then things were more affordable; ten cents would buy an egg and five cents would buy one piece of bread or cookies. We were not always so poor, but my father had died when I was eight, and no one was left to take care of us.

It was that poverty that made me decide eventually to come to the United States. In Mexico, I was making five pesos a day. I would often hear people speak about how much money they earned working in the United States. When I would hear their stories it made me want to come north. My intentions were to go to the United States, make money, and then come back home to Mexico and buy a truck. I wanted to establish a small business in transportation, transporting cargo from one place to another.

But I ended up buying nothing because my mother bought a house, and, in helping her, I forgot about my plan completely. After all, she had no one to look after her, and I did not want my mother to suffer. So my plans were to make money and help my family. It was a difficult decision to venture into the United States because I had always been very close to my family. I felt very sad to have to leave. The first time I crossed the border was especially difficult. I was afraid I was not going to make it back home. I had never been so far from home and so far from my mother. She never did want me to come, but I did. I had to.

I had heard of the Bracero Program from a man with whom I eventually worked making homes in University City. He used to be one of those who came north every so often, and he would tell me of the good money he would make. He would get contracts for forty-five days. So he gave me the idea to come as a contracted worker. I did not want to come illegally because we would hear that the illegals would be imprisoned and treated horribly. At worst, one could die, and no one would even know. It was for that reason that I thought of doing everything legally.

I was in Mexico City the first time I decided to come to work in the United States, so I borrowed money from my sister who lived in Pachuca. From Pachuca, we traveled to Monterrey, Nuevo León and it was there that I was contracted. For one hundred pesos we got our names on a list. For being my first time, I had good luck because, when I got to Monterrey, I did not have any identification; but they believed me when I said I was thirty-one years of age when I was only just twenty years old.

I passed all my medical exams, which included X-rays. I remember they took my blood, but I really do not remember more: it was a long time ago in 1954. We also got sprayed all over with a powder by a machine. It was like talc to kill animals or I do not know what. We were all undressed and sprayed in case we had a certain disease. They took us through Reynosa Tamaulipas to Wellup to pick cotton. From Monterrey to Reynosa we were taken in a cargo train where they transported the cattle.

There were more than 500 of us contracted at Monterrey—a lot of people. The train was packed. We made a five or six-hour trip without restrooms or food. The train car only had barrels of water for us to drink. I worked there for forty-five days picking cotton; I had never done that before, but I learned how very fast. We did not make a lot of money that trip because the cotton was small. We were paid $2.05 for each 100 pounds, and that was only enough to make 10 to 15 dollars a day. When the harvest was over in Texas they took us to St. Louis, Missouri to pick more cotton. I was there for maybe 55 days. I did not make much money there either, but since I spent my money only on food, I was able to take money home when I went back in November.

It was the first, but not the last time I came. Eventually I got contracted a number of times in Mexico City with the government. There they gave us passes to come and be contracted in Emplame, Sonora, or Irapuato. I was contracted in both places, Empalme and Irapuato. Even though we started the process in Mexico City, we had to pay our transportation to the border regions by buses or trains and from there we would be sent to our different destinations. I worked in Santa Paula and Oxnard, picking lemons, walnuts, lettuce barriers, strawberries, and all other types of vegetables.

The work was hard, but we made an honest and humble living. I liked to work. Picking lettuce was probably the most difficult thing to pick because our waists would hurt a lot. The easiest job was also in lettuce, stapling the boxes shut. I could staple sixteen boxes per minute. A person would place the box in front of me and I would staple it "pas...pas...pas." I was fast. I did that for nine months. I liked it. I liked to work. When we picked, I was always the one in the front. The foreman never yelled at me for being behind. That is what they would do if we were slow; they would yell at us to make us work fast. That was perhaps the only injustice—that the work was nonstop. But I never got in trouble because I did as I was told, and I was fast.

Actually I did get in trouble twice for picking fruit that was not yet ripe. They punished me by giving me two days off. But overall, I was a good worker, and they even helped me get my green card by writing letters on my behalf so I could stay here in the United States. Those are good memories—when I got the letters to immigrate. There are good memories, too, of good friends that I made in those years. We did not speak to anyone other than our fellow workers. We spoke only to our bosses when they spoke to us. One time, I remember we went on a strike because they were not paying us enough. The strawberries were small, and we could not pick enough to make a dime. As a result, we were moved to where we could work more and make more.

In all, I came three times—once for forty-five days and then for six months and again for sixteen months. At the end, they would take us to the border and drop us off. We could cross through the gates and take the bus back home to wherever we were from. If you ask me, the program was a good thing for us— the people who were poor. We all benefited from coming north. Some of the old folks came as early as the forties during the war. There was no one here to harvest the crops—they had all gone to war.

It was a good thing for the poor; I had nothing, and I thank the Lord I was able to make something in Mexico and take care of my mother. They say they want more *braceros* to come again. It is because they can pay them less like they did then. That remains to be seen by those who are still alive—for those who have died, it is too late.

José Perez
1957-1964

I decided to go to the United States to find work so I could help my family back home.

José Rodolfo Jacobo

My name is José Pérez Antúnez, and I am from Santa Cruz Villa Gómez, Michoacán. My economic status was very bad in Mexico. They paid us 500 pesos or 50 cents a day. It was barely enough to sustain a family on my ranch. I decided to go to the United States to find work so that I could help my family back home. The news about the Bracero Program traveled from the north by word of mouth, person to person. My family and I thought that my decision to become part of the Bracero Program was a good one because we felt it would help us escape from the poverty.

I was contracted in Empalme, Sonora and then brought to Calexico. I traveled from my homeland to Empalme by bus and from Empalme to United States in a train. My experience in Empalme was between good and bad. My first experience in United States, however, was very good, and that is one of the reasons why I kept returning. Once we crossed the border, they took us to El Centro, California, and that is where they performed the medical examinations.

They gave us physicals to check if we had hernias and they would take X-rays. Another thing they would do when we crossed the border was fumigate us by undressing us completely and then they would throw powder all over our bodies. They also gave us two pairs of clothing in a box and the powder was thrown on the clothes as well. I was not really chosen for the program, in those times when *los coyotes* existed. I had to pay a coyote $150 to be on the list for the Bracero Program.

In my first contract, I was sent to work in Yuba City, California. My first experience working in the United States was reasonable, considering that I was young and a very good worker. I liked coming to California because that was where they paid and treated the braceros the best. There was some exploitation— mostly in the meals. They would charge us for food and give us small meals such as hotdogs. My boss was an Indian (Hindu) and my relationship with him was very good. He liked me because I worked fast and hard.

I remember feeling sad when our contract was over. I was sad because it was hard to get another contract and sometimes it would take a very long time. Another reason it was a difficult time was because I had to pay every time I wanted to reenlist in the Bracero Program. My relationship with my co-workers was good; I never had any problems with them. I also never had problems with my bosses or the Americans. I participated in many contracts from 1957 to 1964. Sometimes I was contracted once and sometimes twice a year depending on the contract they would give me.

At that time, I thought the program was good because one could go home to their ranch, help their family and still have some money left over, but now, I think things are very different; it is not the same. If a new Bracero Program were created, I do not think I would be for it. They say they would bring them only when work is available. With such limited time working, Mexican workers could not make enough money to help themselves like before. It would be too difficult now; why would they come and suffer when they would not be able to help themselves or their family? Even life in Mexico is very expensive now.

José Jesús Jacobo-Páramo

1956

We lacked money, food, housing, clothing—all of that.

José Rodolfo Jacobo

$\mathcal{My}$ name is José Jesús Jacobo. I grew up in a small village called Palo Blanco in the state of Guanajuato.[1] Our childhood in Mexico was a difficult one, but there were many good things we valued and still do value. Compared to life today, life back then was full of suffering; we were very poor we lacked and needed a lot of things. We also worked a lot. When I say we had needs, I am talking mainly about needs associated with economics. We lacked money, food, housing, clothing—all of that. We lived in a rural area, so we needed everything except fresh air. We had plenty of that.

We used to get shoes, a shirt, and a pair of pants after every harvest, assuming there was a harvest. We made sure that our clothes would last the whole year by repairing our shoes and clothes. If a pair of shoes was 15 pesos, but you could fix them for 3 pesos, then you would fix them instead of getting new ones. We extended the life of our shoes and clothes as much as we could. Our meals consisted primarily of beans, chilies and tortillas, and atole in the morning.[2]

We ate what we cultivated. Back then for us, agriculture was not a business but our food. Part of it was because agricultural output was very limited. One barely made enough to survive until the next season, until the next harvest. We cannot say we lived comfortably, but, we had no other choice, and we made the best of what we had. There was nowhere to go. Still, our childhood was a good one despite lacking things that children should have, such as schooling. There was no school. We lacked education; there was none and there were no means for us to go elsewhere.

We did not go to school as children; very few of the children did. What little we learned, we learned from our own interest by asking people who knew how to read to teach us. It was difficult for our parents to teach us since they were always working and,

---

[1] The date of the interview was Monday, June 8, 2002
[2] Atole is a corn drink.

in most cases, our own parents did not know how to read or write themselves. So, we had a difficult time. But we had enough knowledge to survive. We counted with our fingers to keep track of things. It was a different time. People did not even have vehicles. If you had a truck, you were considered very rich and highly respected. We had no political awareness of any kind; we were in the politics of survival. We had no electricity, water, or drainage. We got our water from the ground from natural springs.

If we had money when we got sick, we would go to a doctor—if not to the pharmacy or otherwise, home remedies did the trick. There was no medical assistance of any kind in our village, so we had to go by horse or donkey to the nearest town. There was no other method of transportation. It was difficult, but we were a united family. A united family always gets through hard times. Back then, we respected our elders; we never questioned them. We did what our parents said. If our neighbor complained to my dad about something we did, we were punished. There was no rebellion, no malice. In that regard, our childhood was a good one. We had respect for our elders. The formal respect that existed was nice. Nowadays kids have no respect for their elders.

A holiday for us was to go to town and see people in the plaza. We had no money, so all we could do was see the things that were for sale. It was rare to go to town; it usually happened only after harvest and even then, only one of us could go at a time. We took turns going to town, one Sunday each. There were a lot of kids in my house, so when we were told it was our turn to go to town we even showered with great joy because we were going to Acambaro.[3] That's what excited us—going to town and watching stores and people. We had no radio, no television. There was no form of entertainment other than to maybe play marbles or "al trompo."[4]

---

[3] Acambaro is a town in Guanajuato, Mexico.

[4] A trompo (top) is a toy.

Life for us was mostly about work. As soon as you could walk you were out herding the cattle or goats. We awoke early in the morning, and we did not have to receive instructions; we knew what to do. Depending on age, each one would have a different responsibility, whether it was taking care of goats or cattle or working in the bean and corn fields. We got up and our mother had breakfast for us, and off we went to the hills. That's how it was back then. When I was five years old I took care of the cattle. At fifteen, I was in charge of the oxen because the young ones could not do that. One needed strength to handle the oxen.

I remember one time my older brother and I woke up really early, and, by mistake, we went off to the fields really early. We did not have a clock or a radio. We usually woke up at four o'clock to feed the oxen, as was the custom, and then headed for the fields. But this time there was a full moon, and we went off to work super early. My father was surprised to find that we had finished our work by five o'clock in the morning when he arrived. We had apparently gone to work around midnight thinking it was later in the morning. I never forgot that because we were kids getting up to work without anybody ordering us. There was no malice, no fear—just work.

One of the scariest things we did face was sickness. One time, my younger sister got sick and the pain would not go away. They took her to a pharmacist, but the pain would not go away. I remember feeling very sad. The nights were long, and she was in a lot of pain. I thought she was going to die. I was thirteen years old and felt helpless. We had no money to assure better medical treatment. It was scary when anyone of us got sick.

One time a snake bit me. I was almost done with my work when I saw a bushel of beans with some weeds around it and I went to clear it. When I pulled the weeds, I felt a pain and pulled

---

[5] Fright; in this case it means that he was in a state of shock.

my hand back and hanging from it was a snake. I remember my dad taking it off. It took me almost two months to get on my feet again. Worst yet, I got *espanto* and that took longer to heal.[5] There were a lot of scorpions and snakes.

That was the kind of life we had as children. It was rough. It greatly motivated us to come to *el norte* to seek a better life for our family. But even deciding to go north was no easy decision, because if we did not have money to go to the local town, it was practically impossible to go north to the United States. It was simply out of reach for most of us back then. It is still out of the reach for many in Mexico to come to work in the United States. It is hard to collect 2,500 dollars to pay a coyote.

When I was sixteen years old, I wanted to come to the United States to work. As one of the eldest children I felt I had the responsibility to find a way to help my family. I would have to come illegally however, since legally I could not because of my age. But my father would not accept my coming illegally. I endured one more year until I turned seventeen. Then I altered my birth certificate, allowing me to do my military service through which I could obtain a credential that could be used as a legal document to be contracted as a *bracero*. At that time, the contract centers were in Empalme, Monterrey or Mexico City. The places where one could be contracted often changed. One usually knew by word of mouth or through local government where these were, but those places in the north were constant.

Once I had the military credential and the proper age, (thanks to the altering of my birth documents), I went to Monterrey with hopes of being contracted. We were there fifteen days, and we were not able to do so. There were five of us from the same village, and we all went back to our village, disappointed with our failure. The year was 1956. I went back to the military service in 1957, and in 1958, I tried again to go north. I was now eighteen, and my father gave my older brother and me his blessings to try again. My dad warned us to be good and to be careful. He had been a *bracero* since the early forties. We again went to Monterrey and after eight days there we were contracted. I was sent to Texas with six other friends from the village. We all ended up in Eagle Pass.

I remember that day clearly because I was fighting a cold and I had gone to the doctor who gave me some medicine. But I was sweating profusely all night long, even though it was cold and raining. It rained so much that the buses that were taking us across the border could not cross the Sabine River. We had to find a way to get across because there were buses on the other side of the river waiting for us. After two hours of walking and searching for a good spot to cross, we finally came across a forty-meter area were we felt it was safe to cross the Sabine River.

I was so sick by then that it took two people to get me across. We had to walk two hours back to where the buses were on the other side. We got there about eleven o'clock in the morning. I remember being scared because I felt sick and lonely. I was seventeen years old and, and, for the first time, far away from home. My only consolation was that I had my bother and some friends from the village and, even though they were also scared, at least we were together.

Unfortunately, when we got to La Mesa, Texas, we were separated, and I was sent on my own to a place different from my brother and friends. I was afraid since I was sick. But thank God, I was soon feeling better and working. At the place where we worked, they let us borrow money to buy groceries. I had no idea how to cook, but I did know how to make corn tortillas, and I learned how to do flour ones as well. We helped each other buy and cook food.

Fifteen days after working, we were paid and we went to town. I remember feeling good about myself having earned some dollars. I felt proud. We picked cotton, and were paid a dollar-fifty for one hundred pounds. It was hard work. I was used to working hard, but not that hard. We used to work all day long, from morning to dusk until the foreman would tell us "that's it." We made good money but it was hard-earned money. *Era una buena chinga.*[6]

We were lucky that there were many men who were not able to come across. Some were denied permits because of medical reasons. For them, it was difficult because they had borrowed money to make the trip. It was difficult to save 250 pesos back then to make it to Monterrey, and now they had to go back with no dollars, only their debt. I was lucky: I came three times and got various extensions. The second time I came, I ended up in Arkansas. There I got several extensions, of my permit. Basically, if there was work, you got extensions and when the work was over, you were sent back home. If you were a good worker, you received a letter that said you were good.

The third time I came, I got on a list in Morelia and was sent to Empalme. After two weeks in Empalme, I was sent to Artesia, California to pick strawberries. My contract was for forty-five days, but there was so much work that they kept renewing it, and I ended up staying there six months. At the end of the six months, I got a permit for three months to work at a flower ranch. I was there for a whole year. I came one last time after that to El Centro, California. We did not make money at all there; in fact, we barely made enough to pay for our food. Luckily for me, the rancher I had worked for in Artesia liked my work and arranged it so I could work for him and eventually help me get my papers.[7]

My dreams were to help my family and to make something of my life—to have something: a house, maybe a cow or two, a piece of property. Certainly we wanted to have plenty of food because

---

[6] "It was a good fuckin' job."
[7] Green card.

we had suffered some hunger at times. Many times we did not have enough to eat, not even enough tortillas. We were simply very poor. God be blessed, after that we ate plenty, but we were never satisfied; we continued to work.

We were successful with our first trip. My brother and I were able to help buy a house in our town for our family. The house was an old adobe house without any basic necessities, but the idea was to fix it little by little. Eventually, we had electricity and running water. Back then we worked for our family. We all worked as team. It was a great feeling to buy the house for our family. I remember that first trip I made 9,000 *pesos*, and I bought myself some pants and a shirt. My second trip was not as good; I was only able to buy a set of clothes and one cow.

Working in the United States as a *bracero* was difficult for a number of reasons. Some of the work was hard, even though we were used to that type of work. The short hoe was very hard because we were bent over all day long. Work was hard, but that's what we did, and we were young. We tried to look at all things in a positive way; otherwise, we would make things that were already hard, even harder. There were many city folks who did not make it. They were not used to such work. Others adapted quickly to the demands.

I remember the first time I came. I was picking cotton and I was able to pick between 300 and 350 pounds a day, but there was a guy picking up to 700 pounds per day. I worked really hard and was exhausted at the end of the day, but I could not do more. I knew he had come as a *bracero* before and had experience in picking, so I started working next to him to see what I could learn.

But when one works in those jobs, the moment comes when one gets really tired, and I stood up briefly to rest my back and that is when he told me do not stand. He said if you stand up it will hurt more, and then you will have to stop over and over again. Despite my pain, I listened to him and did not stop to stretch my back at all. That day I picked 600 pounds. He really worked my ass off. The next day I felt I was dying, and I did not work next to him, but I also thought if I picked that much next to him then I should be able to do it by myself. That day I picked 700 pounds. From then on I got better and better until I reached 1,200 pounds which was about 15 to 17 dollars. That was the time I made 9,000 *pesos*.

It is interesting that the hardest people on us were the Mexican foremen. In my last trip we had a Mexican foreman who treated us as if we were nothing. He would always yell at us no matter how hard we worked. Some were definitely nice, but some were very bad. The good ones wanted us to work, but they were not bad. But overall the rancher wanted us because we were good workers. Many times growers asked for us in particular because we were good workers. Usually, if you were recontracted, it was because you were a good worker. Lazy people simply could not make it.

Printed in Mexico
by
IMPREGRAFIC
Tel. (619) 921-1755

Canción Mixteca

(D: A' R')
Canción Ranchera

Que lejos estoy del suelo
donde he nácido,
inmensa nostálgia invade
mi pensamiento.

Y al verme tan solo y triste
cual hoja al viento
quisiera llorar,
quisiera morir de sentimiento.

Oh tierra del sol
suspiro por verte
ahora que lejos
yo vivo sin luz, sin amor.

Y al verme tan solo y triste
cual hoja al viento
quisiera llorar
quisiera morir de sentimiento.

Oh tierra del sol
suspiro por verte
ahora que lejos
yo vivo sin luz, sin amor.

Y al verme tan solo y triste
cual hoja al viento
quisiera llorar,
quisiera morir de sentimiento.